Praise for
SHOES WISELY

For more than a decade, I have known Wendy Treat to be a woman of enduring faith, possessing a true and intense passion for the things of God. She understands how women feel and what it takes to overcome in *a spider-filled world.* Her new book, *Shoes Wisely,* is honest, straightforward and directly from her heart.

> Victoria Osteen
> Senior Pastor, Lakewood Church
> Houston, Texas

Wendy is a woman of integrity when it comes to applying Godly wisdom to everyday life. Her latest book, *Shoes Wisely* promises to be an insightful, helpful and fun read for women and girls whose passion for shoes could well turn them into passionate world changers.

> Bobbie Houston
> Senior Pastor, Hillsong Church
> Sydney, Australia

I LOVE THIS WOMAN!! She has encouraged me personally for SO many years. Wendy has cheered me on from up close AND from afar, in parenting, in ministry, in living life in GODS strength and joy! *Shoes Wisely* is going to be a complete and utter blessing to your life.

> Darlene Zschech
> Singer, Songwriter, Worship leader
> Senior Pastor, Hope Unlimited Church
> NSW, Australia

Shoes Wisely is the best of Wendy Treat in 200 pages! It captures every woman's desire to be a better woman like only Wendy can. This is a book for every woman!

> CeCe Winans
> Gospel Recording Artist

Wendy's new book SHOES WISELY is so wonderful, informative and helpful, if we will just heed it. I salute her for instructing us and teaching us how to stomp on the devil. In fact, it will "knock the socks" off of you.

> Dodie Osteen
> Co-Founder of Lakewood Church
> Houston, Texas

Shoes Wisely is the most creative Christian writing I have seen in years! Dr. Wendy's hilarious, yet practical approach to everyday life through the allegorical illustration of SHOES was brilliant. This is a must read!

> Lisa Osteen Com
> Associate Pastor,
> Author of *You Ar*
> Houston, Texas

Because of her years of experience, Wendy has captured the essence of who women are and what they need, brilliantly in this book, *Shoes Wisely!* I totally identified with every type of shoe (after all we women love shoes), and I was captivated from the first page! I'm already excited for Shoes Wisely #2!

Sharon Kelly
Senior Pastor, Wave Church
Virginia Beach, Virginia

Women can be great multitaskers! We can do three things at once with a smile, yet we can fail to realize each task can require a different shoe. In this brilliant book, Wendy takes each reader on a journey to view the *spiritual shoe room* that is available for their life. With great insight and powerful examples, Wendy's words guide you through the breadth and depth of what each shoe can do! Thank you Wendy for living this book before you wrote it. I pray every woman would choose to pick up a copy of *Shoes Wisely!*

Charlotte Scanlon-Gambill
Pastor, Life Church
Bradford, England

I love this book. I will never look at my shoe closet the same way again. Now I see, "fighting shoes", "dancing shoes", and "faith shoes" AND I know which pair to put on when.

Christine Caine
Founder A21 Campaign

It doesn't surprise me that Wendy would come up with this hilarious, yet brilliant idea to use our SHOES as an illustration of how we can walk through life victoriously. You will love this practical, insightful look at the shoes found in your closet!

Dr. Dee Dee Freeman
Senior Pastor, Spirit of Faith Christian Center
Temple Hills, Maryland

Jesus talked to farmers about farming. He talked to fishermen about fishing. He talked to shepherds about sheep. So it is no surprise that He would talk to a *shoe lover* about shoes. Wendy's adept use of shoes to illustrate important life-lessons will hook you from start to finish. What a better way for women to learn than through shoes?

Joni Lamb
Vice President, DayStar Television

This book is so clever I wish I would have thought of it! Now, I'm thinking to myself, "Did I shoes wisely there?" "Am I wearing the right shoes now?" Thank you, Wendy for teaching us women how to think outside of the (shoe) box!

Vickie Winans
Recording Artist/Comedian

If you love shoes, like me, you will not be able to put this book down. I can really relate to the, "boxing shoes", "stiletto shoes", and I love those "stomping boots!" This is a book for all the girls in your life!

Sheila Walsh
Author of, *God Loves Broken People*
and Those Who Pretend They're Not.

Shoes Wisely is an exciting must read, as you are experiencing the thrills of zip lining with Wendy, to the strong faith walk she takes fighting against cancer. You will, laugh, cry, be encouraged, and feel like her best friend, as she helps you put on the right shoes for the right moments as we climb, dance, and run our race, pressing forward to our high calling in Christ. Dr. Wendy is a leader among leaders, and will help you rise higher than you ever thought you could go!

Desiree Ayres,
Co-Pastor of In His Presence Church
Author of *Beyond the Flame*
Woodland Hills, California

Some of the most beautiful shoes I've seen Wendy wear you'll never "see" on her feet or "find" in her closet! Wendy and I were flying overseas to minister just days after her mom passed away. The moment the stewardess came to our row, Wendy's *Love Shoes* went on. The hurt and pain of losing her mom was real, the tears were flowing, but her love for people and her passion for seeing each person come to know Him was greater than the ache in her heart. Wendy lovingly shared with her God's love, and by the time our plane landed our stewardess was a changed person. You will be changed too after reading, *Shoes Wisely*.

Marguerite Reeve
Pastor, Faith Community Church
West Covina, California

"Shoes Wisely" captured me from the very first page. I felt like I was sitting down and having a personal conversation with Wendy and gleaning from her amazing down-to-earth wisdom. This is a book I can't wait to tell my friends about!

Holly Wagner
Senior Pastor, Oasis Christian Center
Los Angeles, California
Author of *Warrior Chicks* and *Daily Steps for GodChicks*

Shoes Wisely

Choosing the Right Shoe
for Every Occasion

DR. WENDY TREAT

This book is dedicated to my best girls; my daughters and my granddaughter:

Tasha, Christa, and Willow.

Together we will stomp through the hard seasons and dance

through the fun ones! Through it all, there is no greater joy than doing

life with you. You make me proud to be your mom and grandma.

Together we Shoes Wisely!

SPECIAL THANKS

I Corinthians 12:14-20, talks of how the many members of the Body of Christ each does its part. I am so thankful for these amazing people, who have not only done their part, but continually go the extra mile to give and truly serve the Body of Christ. Thank you for sharing your talents with me and the many women who will benefit from reading, *Shoes Wisely!*

Terry Schurman

Molly Venzke

Tasha Masitha

Charlotte Jennings

Debbie Willis

Jocelyn Frasier

Lisa Garrison

Sheri Blumburg

Kris Hillstrom

Jordan Wesolek

Sean Bollinger

Anna Groves

Fahren Johnson

David Rafael

Katie Coronado

And finally, I want to thank the wonderful men in my life,
Casey, Caleb, Moses and Micah.
I am constantly inspired by you all.

Shoes Wisely: Choosing the Right Shoe For Every Occasion
ISBN#1480180564 (10) 978-1480180567 (13)
Copyright (c) 2013 by Wendy Treat
Casey Treat Ministries. All Rights Reserved
Product #8044

Published by
Casey Treat Ministries
P. O. Box 98800
Seattle, WA 98198
www.caseytreat.com
www.wendytreat.com

Cover Design: Tasha Masitha and Kris Hillstrom
Graphic Artist: Lisa Garrison
Sketch Artist: David Rafael
Cover Photo: Kris Hillstrom

CONTENTS

INTRODUCTION

The idea for *Shoes Wisely* was born in my heart one day as I was out riding my bike. I was just peddling along, enjoying a magnificent Northwest spring morning, when the whole concept just popped into my head. Imagine using *shoes* to illustrate our daily walk as women – from sneakers to heels to dancing shoes - the possibilities were endless. And so, this book was born.

Shoes Wisely is a book about women - for women. It is for women of all ages...from young to old; professional women to stay-at-home moms; women who have strong self-images to women who don't know where they fit in. For the women who could use practical tips on how to live a life that sometimes seems unreachable. The women who say, *You know I can't, it's too hard, and it's just not fun anymore.*

As women, we feel so much of the burden of life. We carry the load of responsibility - taking care of not only our home, but our marriage, and our children. Plus, for today's woman, we often have a career we need to focus on, measure up to, and succeed at. Then, on top of that, we have us! We try to take care of ourselves, making sure we look just right, act just right, and in the end, we can never, ever measure up.

The challenge of womanhood is measuring up. Often seeing ourselves as failures in all those areas where we are *just not good enough.* Trying to measure up and just not seeing how we will do it. If we conquer one area, it seems something else pops up right behind it.

Personally, I have walked through many seasons of life, in many pairs of shoes. I am no longer the 20-year-old who is the youngest in the group. I'm no longer the 30-year-old or the 40-year-old. Now I'm in the over 50's group. I have experienced the good and the bad of life. Although I have been successful in my marriage, my family and my ministry, I can still sometimes feel the burden of not measuring up. It can all seem so overwhelming.

On top of that we get to be a certain age and we start gaining weight. We just want to say, *really?* We didn't like our body when we were 20, then suddenly we're 40 and then we are pushing 60. We wonder how that happened!

Through the years, as I have sought out answers for myself, I have found the peace that comes from God's Word. I have found the answer that only comes from a place inside; a place that the world cannot touch. I have found a deep sense of *I can do this,* that is only found inside of God's ways.

In finding those answers for myself, I have a deep desire to share them with you. I want to shed some light on how we, as godly women, can be *soul healthy* in a world that is forever telling us we are not okay. If we are going to do more than just make it through another day, we need to get real. We need to talk about how to deal with our marriages, when sometimes we think, *Are you kidding me – did you really just fart in the room? I mean, really? And you burped too?* Those kinds of issues are so practical and yet if we can talk about them, and make them funny, instead of irritating, maybe we can make our marriages healthier, happier, and even, in some cases, make them last.

I want you to know that, like you, I live a real life, too. I live with stress, and disappointments and hurts just like you. Just like you, I try to live my life in a way that brings about a sense of victory. I need to have laughter in my life, and walk with a spirit of joy.

So, how can we walk in joy when our husband toots when he shouldn't, and burps when he really shouldn't, and forgets something that we wanted him to remember? Then, our friend, the one we thought would be there, is not there for us because she is going through a challenging season of life and is being weird. To top it off our kids are being disrespectful and frustrating...again!

When the world comes crashing down and we feel defeated, we don't have to give in. We can change the standard. We can become women who rise up and truly live in a way that brings us peace and a spirit of joy. As we do this, we can draw in other women who need what we have.

Let's go on this journey together to discover God's ways of dealing with life. Whether you are a girl, who at age 16 is just walking into womanhood, or an amazing great-grandmother, who will get a chuckle from the memory of some of these situations, we can all benefit from what God has in store for us through the *wisdom of shoes!*

Love you much!

Wendy Treat

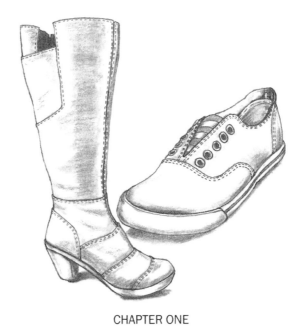

CHAPTER ONE

Choose Your Shoes

Choose Your Shoes

Women and shoes just seem to go together! Every woman wants more shoes, right?! Shoes are universal. We can be skinny as a rail or we can be a little bit over our weight limit, but we can still buy ourselves a great pair of shoes. Most women love to look at shoes; we see a magazine and look at the shoes, we walk into a department store and we go to the shoe section, because even when nothing else in the store fits us, we can always get a new pair of shoes!

When you first see a woman her shoes tell you so much about her. There are happy shoes, play shoes, work shoes, hiking shoes, exercise shoes, worn-out shoes, and there are, *Oh my goodness, how can you walk in those,* shoes! There are glittery shoes, there are plain shoes, there are short shoes, tall shoes...so many shoes, and they all represent us, as women, in some way.

Personally, I have to admit, I love shoes! So much so, that I could possibly be considered a *shoe-aholic* in some circles. I love wearing them, but even more, I think, *I love looking for them.* There is this one online shoe sale site – and I am kind of addicted to it. At one time I seriously had to ban myself from buying the shoes...but I didn't ban myself from looking at them! At times, if I am just feeling *ho hum,* I will go online just to look at the shoes! How weird is that?! I just look at all of the beautiful shoes. I don't buy any, I just look. I like them. They just speak to my heart. It makes me feel happy!

What Are Your Shoes Saying About You?

Let's admit it, many of us women come into an environment, and everybody looks at everybody else's shoes. That is usually one of the first things we look at. We look at their shoes and it tells us something about that woman. What kind of shoes is she wearing? High, low, fancy...I feel that *shoes* speak a language we women can all relate to. When we look at others' shoes, we form a thought about that person. We know whether she takes care of herself by the way she takes care of her shoes. Are they worn down, scuffed, need some polish? Are her shoes beautiful, practical, do they match her outfit? It's amazing how much a woman's shoes will tell us about her...in about 10 seconds flat!

Our shoes also tell us something about ourselves. When we go to put on our shoes, we have some sort of thought or feeling about them. We consider our day, our plans, how we feel, what we want to accomplish, and choose our shoes accordingly. Is our day going to be busy or slow? Do we want to impress or stay in the background?

There are some women – one in particular - whom I can hardly wait to see, because she has the most amazing, incredible shoes. I look forward to seeing her every time because it just makes me happy to see her pretty shoes.

I can tell she loves to take care of herself, and she gets joy out of how she presents herself. And her joy is contagious!

All of that is important and great, but the most important message I see when I consider the message of shoes is this: *there are all different kinds of shoes;* a vast variety, but no one can say, *This is THE SHOE!* We don't get to say, *I will only wear this color shoe.* Or, *I will only love this type of shoe. I will only love this shoe if it has a flower on it or this one because it sparkles.*

No, what we find is that people need a variety of shoes. We all must have the beauty and practicality of all the different kinds of shoes in our lives. In the same way, we are all created equal before God. He doesn't look at the color of our skin. He does not judge if we are young or old; if we are skinny or if we are fat. He looks at each one of us as an individual. He sees the beauty of each person.

When we look at the creation of humanity, we see all the looks and all the beauty of what God has done...from the ageing one, who has the beauty of experience and wisdom written in the lines of her face, to the fresh beauty of a newborn, with her perfectly smooth skin and soft innocence. They both show the range of beauty in God's creation.

Look at the Beauty of God's Creation

From the abundance of my heart, I have to say, there is no race to be ignored or put down. There is not an age of a person that is to be despised. God looks at us as daughters and says, *Come on now. Don't judge by what society says our outside should look like, only look at the beauty that I have created.* Look at every person and you will see the beauty and creativity of God. His handiwork is on display over and over as we look at all the colors, sizes, shapes, and personalities of women...all of us unique, all of us *designer!*

I think about the beauty of women, from the newborn, to the pimply face of the darling teenage girl who is walking into womanhood, to the woman who is in the midst of marriage and motherhood, and then sooner than she thinks she is getting hot flashes. Sadly, we have not valued all the varieties of seasons; all the looks and ages. We have somehow missed valuing the many extremely important seasons of life. We have made some of them bad instead of beautiful.

I am so excited about this great visual - which I believe is from the heart of God - for us to love and appreciate all looks. We need to recognize there are different *shoes* for different seasons. Instead of resisting and getting depressed, let's applaud each season as it comes. Instead of thinking, *this shoe must only have this height;* why not realize that would be true for a particular season, but another shoe might have a different height for a different season.

We become truly successful women when we learn to applaud others, and not compare ourselves or our season with someone else's. We can rejoice with our sister, who is in a season we are not yet in, but also rejoice in ourselves, too. Why not enjoy who we are and run our race, instead of always comparing ourselves to someone else.

Life is Not Stagnant

We need to realize that life is not stagnant. We don't stay in the same place forever. We have been created to flex with the various roles we play within each situation or season of life. We need to be able to switch up our shoes to fulfill whatever is needed at that particular moment. Many times we limit ourselves and God by becoming stuck in a thought of what we want to be, what we want to look like, or what we want to be perceived as. But, as I said, that is so limiting.

The truth is, we will need to change our shoes all of our lives. When we were kids we wore little kids shoes; and then as we grew, we wore shoes that fit our new season of life. Not only do we need to change our size of shoes, but we change the style as we mature and grow. That is the best picture - one of constant change.

We all start off with little baby shoes – soft little nothing shoes - and then as we continue throughout our lives we add more types of shoes into our closet. As a young mother, raising my three kids, I was constantly changing shoes. First thing in the morning I had on my slippers. The slipper shoes were my casual moments – let's call it the hugs and snuggles of life. It was that cuddly and warm time when I was just *mom*. No rush, no pressure, just that time to *be*.

That was for a short *season* of my day. As the day progressed, I would get up and put on my tennis shoes. It was the time of day to get busy and stay in shape! It was time to switch up those shoes and get to work – not only physically, but mentally as mom, in leading my household. My tennis shoes represent taking care of myself and my family. I made a deliberate plan to keep myself in shape and I *put on* those shoes each day.

There are so many different kinds of shoes to represent the many aspects of our day. We put on our Nike tennis shoes, the kind with the big old bottoms, to really attack things in the physical realm. Or maybe we put on our running shoes to quickly go through the chores of the day. Then what about our tiny little Sketchers shoes, because we are going to go shopping and want something really comfortable to wear.

As the day goes on, sometimes we will need to put on our *nursing shoes*. Why? Because one of our children just fell down and needs some attention. Or, maybe *we* fell down and we need some healing for ourselves. Maybe we need to put on our *nursing shoes* because we received a medical diagnosis that we personally or our family has to deal with. Or, one morning we wake up and are sneezing all day. We just know when we have to put on our *nursing shoes*. What are our *nursing shoes?* By the stripes of Jesus I am healed! Our *nursing shoes* represent the wisdom of what to do in that particular situation as sickness tries to attack us or our family.

As our day goes on, there are many other types of *shoes* we will wear. When your husband walks in the door don't forget to trade your *mommy shoes* for your *stiletto shoes,* baby! Your man is home! Then again, there are times he will walk in the door and you don't want to put on your *stiletto shoes.* You actually want to put on your *walking shoes,* because it's time to go for a walk together and talk. It's time for a visit!

In putting on our wifely *walking shoes* sometimes we just need to connect with our husband. It's not the right time for our tennis shoes and it's not the time to put on those stiletto shoes, we just need a comfortable pair of shoes to help us to connect.

Let's not forget our *dancing shoes!* We all need to enjoy those moments where we are dancing, twirling around and just having so much fun. We really do need times of joy and laughter. In the midst of the seriousness of life we often forget our dancing shoes; we forget to be joyful...on purpose. As we experience the total abandon of putting on our dancing shoes, it helps us – at least for the moment - to let go of the stress in our life.

There are so many kinds of shoes that we will be touching on in the pages ahead. I hope you will be encouraged to see your life from a different perspective. I also pray you will renew your thoughts about certain issues in your life and begin fresh in areas that have challenged you in the past.

No Regrets

Our goal is to live life to the fullest. As women, we always want to nurture others, and a good part of our time is spent achieving that goal. At the same time, we don't want to come to the end of our lives filled with regrets. It's so easy for us to pour ourselves out to meet whatever need is most urgent or whatever makes us feel most valuable or important. But, we can easily establish a pattern...one that we don't want or even like. Like a freight train traveling a hundred miles an hour, we just can't seem to stop.

The patterns we allow ourselves to establish in our days can turn into weeks, which will often turn into months and years. Sometimes those patterns bring great satisfaction and success, but they can also bring failure. This is because we brought something into our day, our week, our month, our year that should never have been brought in. Habits can easily become *the way we always do it,* without any thought for what God wants us to do.

The established patterns and disciplines in our life really do matter. We either do or do not read the Word of God. We either pray and talk to God, or we do not. We are either planted in our church, or we are not. We have to consciously decide what positive disciplines we want to establish in our lives. Then, we decide how we can keep ourselves fresh in every new season by re-thinking and re-establishing those patterns.

We can also, inadvertently, allow ourselves to create patterns of heaviness in our homes. Sometimes there isn't anything that is terribly wrong; we are simply wearing the wrong shoes. We can't create the right actions when we wear the wrong shoes over and over and over and over and over. We don't think about what we are doing, we just keep wearing the wrong shoes for too long. We need to change those shoes!

Wisdom to Make a Change

Runners will understand this – because they know the value of their shoes. A really committed runner will go to a specialty shoe store to get their shoes fit just right for their foot. It's important because those shoes, fitted just right, are extremely important to their success. But, smart runners also understand that those shoes will only be their best for a certain length of time.

Many things in life start out like that. We start out with the right thing at the beginning, but we don't always have the wisdom to make needed changes as time goes on. We started with the right thing, but then we just kept at it. We didn't reassess. We didn't stop to re-evaluate the situation. We didn't stop and say, *Well sheesh, these shoes no longer have the cushion they once did. They no longer have the support I need. They have worn out on the inside.* They eventually start ripping apart on the inside, and this happens in our lives as well.

It takes most of us awhile to realize we are in a new season. We didn't notice a change had happened while we were busy living life. And, it's funny how we want to hold on to what is comfortable; what we have always done before. We love putting on our favorite pair of shoes, but guess what?! That favorite pair of shoes should have been thrown out a long time ago. Literally! Get rid of them!! They no longer belong in our life – or in our closet. It's time to get a new pair of shoes.

No Two Alike

It just amazes me the incredible variety of new shoes available today. When we really look around, how many people are actually wearing the same kind of shoes? Almost none!! If we see somebody with the same pair of shoes on it is almost shocking. Think about this: we could literally line up all the women who are wearing a simple pair of black flats at church one Sunday and they would most likely all be wearing different brands – no two would be alike. It is amazing to me that thousands of women in the same room would rarely be seen wearing the same style of shoes.

How unique is it that we could all live in the same area, within the same town, go to the same stores, and yet we would find such diversity in how obviously different our choices would be. Doesn't that illustration just amaze you? It is mind boggling to think about the uniqueness of each individual and how God created us all to be so completely different. The Bible says in Luke 12:7, *But the very hairs of your head are all numbered. Do not fear therefore; you are of more value than many sparrows.*

He knows us. He *really* knows you...and me! It gives me a sense of strength, knowing that my personality and choices are so unique that I don't even pick out the same things you pick out. You may pick out things that are similar, but there is no one with exactly the same taste.

Similar, Yet Unique

I sometimes laugh because Tasha, my daughter, and I will often show up some place and have a very similar look. She's married and doesn't live at home anymore, but recently we both showed up to work, and I looked at her and she looked at me and we both just started to laugh. We both had on black and white striped shirts with black pants. We both had high, fancy shoes, and a very similar style of jewelry. We looked at each other and just started laughing.

This happens on a regular basis because we have similar taste. But even though we are similar, we are also very different. You could look at us and laugh – both of us ended up looking like we had planned to match that day. But, even though we both had on very similar clothing, we were not the same. She added her flair to it; I added my flair to it and you have something unique.

So it is true with every single one of us. God has given us each a unique quality. We each have a certain type of flair in the style of who we are. You were designed to stand out and enjoy who God has called you to be. Just as there are many, many types of shoes, so it is also true of us...we are each a uniquely designed daughter of God. We have been created to reflect His beauty to the world.

CHAPTER TWO

Pre-Shoe Prayer

Pre-Shoe Prayer

There is just something about being *barefoot* on a warm sandy beach or walking on a beautiful lawn of fresh cut grass. It makes us feel fresh and alive. What better way to portray how we come before God in prayer? We come before Him vulnerable and open, exposing our very hearts and souls; in a sense, we come barefoot.

Remember when God spoke to Moses from the burning bush? God told Moses he was to take off his shoes, for he was standing on holy ground. *Then He said, Do not draw near this place. Take your sandals off your feet, for the place where you stand is holy ground* (Exodus 3:5). There is something about coming to God bare. We have to have a certain kind of vulnerability and openness, a simple innocence when we humble ourselves before God in prayer.

Now, you might think, *that's okay,* but there isn't much to being barefoot. But, if we really think about it, being barefoot comes with more looks than we might first imagine. As we look at a few bare feet, we may see beautiful, polished toenails on one pair of feet, but we might also see toenails that are ragged and not manicured at all on another pair. We may see feet that have walked in the mud and have dirt all over them. There are soft, beautifully cared for feet. There are also feet which have not been cared for at all.

The Feet No One Ever Sees

So imagine *your feet* in all their different looks – the ones that most people don't ever see. This is much like our prayer-life with God. There are times when we come to God and feel very rough. Our feet have been in the mud and have gotten crusty, rough and need exfoliation. They are not beautiful at all! This is the time when we really need to come to God in prayer. We have something happening in our life at the moment and we are in a tough spot. We come before God even with our feet a mess, because prayer is vulnerability. It is coming to Him with all of our imperfections.

Some people think they need to come to God dressed in their best outfit; they think everything about themselves has to be perfect. Their hair has to be all done. Their makeup must be immaculate. They put on beautiful shoes, and they tiptoe in to God with everything all *done.*

That is not our Father God's desire for us. His desire is that we come to Him as we are, even with crusty feet! He wants us to come before Him undone; our toenails can be jagged and unfiled. I know that sounds yucky, but we really need to see this picture. God doesn't expect us to come with perfection. He wants us just as we are.

Prayer Is Just Conversation with God

Many times our prayer life is not working because there is no vulnerability. Prayer is a *conversation* between us and God. It is a time to sit in His presence and talk to our Father. The Bible says in Hebrews that we are to come boldly to the throne of God to receive grace and mercy. *For we do not have a High Priest who cannot sympathize with our weaknesses, but was in all points tempted as we are, yet without sin. Let us therefore come boldly to the throne of grace, that we may obtain mercy and find grace to help in time of need* (Hebrews 4:15-16).

Many of us, when we think of God and prayer, don't think of grace, mercy, and certainly not boldness. We come to God timid and afraid. We cower before this big old God, who we think is going to thump us when we are bad. But, Hebrews says we are to boldly come to Him, and when we do we will receive grace and mercy.

Jagged Toenails Prayer

When I think about having *jagged toenails prayer*, I think about the times when I have approached God in great despair. We all have times when we are devastated and need to rely on the strength of God to help us deal with situations. We all have times of despair when we need to cry out to God.

Recently a couple in our church lost their son in a tragic accident. The extreme sorrow of that situation just makes me cry. I feel such enormous sadness for them and their family. It is the most awful thing that can happen to a parent. And as a parent, I feel that pain. And, I talk to God about that. I go to Father God and say, *God, I am in pain over this situation. Father God, I don't know what to do with what is going on in these people's lives. Please help me Holy Spirit, be my Comforter right now.*

33

I have felt this type of pain many times in my life. Being a Christian since I was seventeen years old, and in the ministry since I was 22, I have experienced some unimaginable situations. From my life, to my children's lives, my husband's life, and my friends' lives there have been many painful times. I have had very close, personal friends have to face every situation from the death of husbands, divorce, financial ruin, to those who have lost their children.

Too often we try to carry the pain of our own lives or the lives of those we care about. More than likely, we all know someone who has lost everything recently; from the terrible natural disasters we have experienced, to the financial crisis, we have all been touched in some way. From people losing their jobs, to losing their homes – we try to carry the burden of all this pain without going to our God. But, He is there all the time. And He is saying to us, *I will give you grace and mercy. I will give you strength. I am your strength; let Me help you deal with the weight of this situation.* It's just too heavy for us to carry alone.

Come Boldly To Our Father God

We need to learn to come boldly to Him, not afraid that He is going to thump us or judge us. Our Father God says to call on Him. He wants us to look to Him as our *Daddy God* – The Bible calls Him our *Abba Father*. It can sometimes be hard for us to think of God in such intimate terms. Many of us have not been raised to see God as good and loving. We hear about the God who destroys and judges with terrible disasters. They even put clauses in our insurance policies about acts of God destroying things. Do we really see God as a destroyer? That is the picture some people have of Him.

Another reason we can't see God as our Daddy is because we have never had a great *earthly father*. Our dad was not a nice guy, and we think of God in the same way. If we want to have a true relationship with God, we have to embrace a different way of thinking. We need to renew the spirit of our minds and begin to understand who our Father God is.

If we want to see who God really is, all we need to do is to look at the beauty all around us. All of creation displays the character of God. How could God destroy the very beauty He has created? That just doesn't make any sense. The amazing creation of God on this earth reflects the beauty, the bigness, the vastness, and the abundance of God. Look at the mountains, the ocean, all the flowers and the trees. There is beauty all around us and it communicates a portion of who He is.

If you doubt, look around and remind yourself that you are talking about The Creator of all this beauty. Our loving Father God who sent His Son to die for us says, *Come to Me, all you who labor and are heavy laden, and I will give you rest* (Matthew 11:28). Life is full of weary times, and the devil does not ever give up. He comes against us in our finances, in our health, in our family life, and in our emotional life. He comes to bring weariness, and to hinder us from walking barefoot before God in our prayer shoes. He has had a successful day if he can keep you from spending intimate time with God in prayer.

He Will Give You Rest

Prayer...that amazing, peaceful place where you and I can run to our Abba Father and confide in Him saying, *Father, I am weary*. And He always says, *Come unto Me, my daughter and I will strengthen you. I will give you rest and peace.* I love how this scripture in Isaiah also tells us how much God wants us to bring Him our burdens and let Him give us His peace: *Or let him take hold of My strength, that he may make peace with Me; and he shall make peace with Me* (Isaiah 27:5).

Many of us will spend our weeks, our months, and our years with no peace. We continually walk in a barren wasteland where there are no answers, no joy, and no peace. We do not understand what it means to walk barefoot into the throne room of God and be completely vulnerable before Him. We can't imagine saying, *Hey God, here I am. I've got my dirty feet and my jagged toenails, and I really need your help.*

When we allow ourselves to get to that place of honesty and vulnerability, God's response is, *Come here, sweetheart. Sit on my lap. Let Me refresh you.* Prayer is that simple. It is simply talking to God. It is taking the time to have an intimate, sweet conversation with God. We don't need to say just the right thing, or be able to speak certain religious words. There are those we can watch and learn about prayer from, but there are also people who pray just to put on a great show. Don't feel intimidated by how others pray; talk to God the way you talk to anyone else – simple, honest, loving.

Powerful Prayer

One thought about powerful prayer: The best way to learn how to pray is to be around sincere Christians who know how to pray. One of the things we stress at Christian Faith Center, the church my husband and I pastor, is to *pray God's Word.* It is important to learn God's Word and as we pray, present it back to God. Your prayers should be based on God's Word, but remember, more importantly, your prayers should communicate *your heart* to God; He does not worry about the *style* in which you communicate.

If you'd like to learn how to use scriptures during your prayer time, I encourage you to get our book, *God's Word for Every Circumstance*. In it we have listed specific scriptures by topic. This is a great tool to use during your prayer time to help with any situation you are facing. When I speak God's Word in my prayer life, I say something like this: *Father God, Your Word says that by His Stripes I was healed! You said it and I'm going to believe it. I believe You took my sickness on the cross and I receive my healing, in Jesus Name, Amen.* It's just that simple. I look for what the Word has to say, and then I remind God of His promises in my conversation with Him. That's prayer!

We need to know that God doesn't ignore us if we don't say everything in just the right order or use King James English. He also doesn't care if we use words that would be considered street words. God understands all languages and forms of expression. I've even heard people pray and inadvertently use cuss words while they were praying. Do you think God doesn't hear and answer them as well? Why not?

Why wouldn't God answer them? God understands that person's language and *the roughness of their feet.* He's not worried! He doesn't get all nervous when we get a little rough around the edges. He's heard it all, and it doesn't matter. Let me say it again: He cares about your heart! He is listening to our *hearts,* not to all the *words* we use to express it!

Praying in the Holy Spirit

Another very important part of being barefoot and vulnerable before God is praying in the Holy Spirit. If we want to be successful Christians on this earth, we must understand the value of being filled with the Holy Spirit. In Romans 8 and I Corinthians 14 are found two very powerful scriptures that tell us what happens as we pray in the Holy Spirit. *Likewise the Spirit also helps in our weaknesses. For we do not know what we should pray for as we ought, but the Spirit Himself makes intercession for us with groaning's which cannot be uttered* (Romans 8:26).

This verse says that as we pray in the Holy Spirit, we are praying the perfect will of God. This verse also teaches us that when we pray in the Spirit, we pray for what we know not. We are praying God's perfect will in our own unique prayer language. Here is that same verse from The Message Bible:

Meanwhile, the moment we get tired in the waiting, God's Spirit is right alongside helping us along. If we don't know how or what to pray, it doesn't matter. He does our praying in and for us, making prayer out of our wordless sighs, our aching groans. He knows us far better than we know ourselves, knows our pregnant condition, and keeps us present before God. That's why we can be so sure that every detail in our lives of love for God is worked into something good (Romans 8:26).

Also, I Corinthians tells us that when we pray in the Holy Spirit our spirit is praying. We don't understand it with our natural mind, but we do it! As we obey God, this powerful gift of prayer releases the will of God into those situations we don't know how to pray for.

For if I pray in a tongue, my spirit prays, but my understanding is unfruitful. What is the conclusion then? I will pray with the spirit, and I will also pray with the understanding. I will sing with the spirit, and I will also sing with the understanding (I Corinthians 14:13-15).

How important this is! As we live our lives on earth, unexplainable things will happen. We all walk through situations that we do not understand, but God gives us the ability, through our prayer language, to pray for those things. We don't know why certain things may be happening in our lives or even how to pray for different situations. We don't know how to pray for a person, but God has given us this amazing prayer language of the Spirit that goes beyond our intellect. It exceeds our natural understanding, so in our time of great need, not knowing what to do, we can pray for those things beyond our knowledge in the natural realm.

Let Jesus Wash Your Feet

One of the most vulnerable parts of being barefooted is to let someone touch and wash your dirty feet. God shows us by Jesus' example how intimate a relationship He wants with us...He want us to come to Him with our dirty, road-travelled, weary feet. Let's look at what Jesus did in this amazing story from the book of John. *So when He had washed their feet, taken His garments, and sat down again, He said to them, "Do you know what I have done to you?* (John 13:12).

I know we talk about Jesus washing the disciples' feet. But, if you really think about it, the Savior of the world bowed down in the posture of a servant and washed their dirty, funky feet. He kneeled before each one of them, took a bowl of water and cleaned each of their feet from the junk and dirt that was all over them.

Our God is not intimidated, nor is He afraid of the junk through which we walk. He doesn't shy away from touching us to help us get rid of all the grime and dirt that clings to us as we walk through our daily lives. He does not shield Himself from our humanity, but instead is touched with our infirmities. He is touched because He is our *Abba Father*, and we are His children.

Any mama who is reading this understands what they, as a parent, are willing to do for their child. You and I don't even blink when we have to change our child's diaper, clean his or her nose, or wash them up when they have all kinds of crud on them. We probably would not do that for another child, but when it's ours, we will take care of business.

Likewise, you are God's child! So when you go to God in prayer, don't think of going with all of your finery on...come to Him in your most vulnerable state...barefoot. Let Him know you. Just like a little child, let yourself relax in His loving arms and be at peace.

Prayer Tips

Just as when we don't have time to do more than give our feet a quick rinse, a quick prayer is also sometimes necessary. Don't feel bad if all you have time for is a quick prayer. We all have those unexpected moments when we have an urgent need; that unexpected moment when we don't know what to do except cry out to our Heavenly Father. I can't tell you how many times I would sneak into the bathroom when my kids were small and close the door pleading, *Father God, please help me.* I was in the midst of chaos and challenges and that was all the time I had.

God recognizes when we have time to just come in for a quick rinse. That isn't a problem once in a while. But, if you always run in and run out, what does that say about your relationship? In our daily earthly relationships, if we only ran into the room and said, *I need this,* and then ran out, how deep would that relationship be? How much value are you putting on that relationship if that was all you ever did?

Prayer to me is talking to God every day, every moment and at any time, whether it is long or short. Smith Wigglesworth once said, *I have not prayed more than 30 minutes in my life, but I have never gone more than 30 minutes without prayer.* I have remembered that all of my Christian life. To me, that is the spirit of a prayer warrior.

That portrays the spirit of a woman who recognizes her life is based on walking with God, every day, all day. We are consumed with making the ways of God and the character of God a part of who we are. We never want to step far away from hearing the voice of God. Daily prayer keeps us in touch with the things of God. Whether we come to Him for a quick prayer, or we linger longer with Father God, it is important we pray on a daily basis. I love this verse in Thessalonians which instructs us to pray without ceasing:

Rejoice always, pray without ceasing, in everything give thanks; for this is the will of God in Christ Jesus for you (1 Thessalonians 5:16-18).

We can pray without ceasing because our access to the Father is unlimited. We all have different needs at different times, but He is always there, waiting to hear and help us. When I talk about not going 30 minutes without prayer, I am saying this; as I drive down the road and happen to see a bad situation, I pray. When I see something negative in the news, I pray. When a friend tells me about a problem in their life or someone else's life, I pray. When I see a need, I don't wait for *my prayer time to pray*. I take that moment and pray for them right then.

Regardless of your need or how much time you have to spend with Father God, never be ashamed to walk into His presence in your bare feet. Don't be ashamed to come to Him with your needs and with your open heart. Your bare feet show how much you need His help, His strength, and His healing touch to penetrate every area in your life.

Come to God with your funky, dirty feet, and let Him wash them, so when you walk out they are clean again. We can walk into prayer wearing the stress and pains of life...and we walk out covered in grace and mercy. Our feet are once again clean, because we have been in the presence of God. We lay our burdens at the feet of Jesus, and we come out clean and whole. That is what prayer is all about!

CHAPTER THREE

These Boots Are Made for Stomping

These Boots Are Made for Stomping

Years ago, when Casey and I took our first mission trip to the Philippines, I got a revelation of the *stomping kind of boots!* One of the first things we learned from our hosts was, as you walked into a room you would first, open the door, next, turn on the light, and finally, you would stomp your foot! And then we would hear the scurry of little critters running into their hiding places. Not a fun sound!!

So, when I think of that trip and how I would stomp my foot to chase away those little critters, it gives me such a great visual of this type of shoe in our lives. Sometimes we just need to get things GONE in our lives. That's when we get out our *stomping boots!*

There are moments in life when there are *critters* all around. We will always run into situations that make us want to run and hide. It's natural to want to run from the scary moments of life. Run from, *I don't think I can do this,* because certain things can kind of give us the willies! How many women really want to go tackle that big old spider in the corner?

Put Your Foot Down!

But, guess what? In life there are *spiders in the corner.* We have, however, a choice of who we will be when those moments come along. Will you be the stomping kind of woman; one who has the faith to stand strong on the Word of God for your family? When your child has an issue at school, are you going to cower? Are you going to be afraid? Or will you put your foot down and say, *Wait a minute. I'm not going to let this happen.*

You may not know how you are going to do it, or even know that you *can* do it in the natural, but something on the inside makes you stomp your foot and say, *I am going to overcome this!* Ephesians 6:10 teaches us, *Finally, my brethren (sisters), be strong in the Lord and in the power of His might.* The Bible also teaches us in 2 Timothy 2:1, *You therefore, my son (daughter), be strong in the grace that is in Christ Jesus.*

As I spend time studying my Bible, I always look for patterns. A pattern is something God says more than once. In some instances He repeats something many times to teach us the importance of certain behaviors or ways of thinking. The word *strong* is used in the Bible 255 times. The word *strength* is used 242 times. God's instruction for us, found consistently from Genesis to Revelation, is to be strong. I think God has a message for us as He says again and again, *be strong!*

Stompin' Kind of Boots

When I think about the *stomping kind of boots,* I think of strong faith. I think of a woman with the stomping kind of personality. W*ell, that sounds just* *great,* you might say, *but I don't know how to be strong like that! I am just not a naturally strong person.* So how do we, be strong? It's easy to assume that to be a *stomping-kind-of-faith* woman you have to be really, really loud. It has nothing to do with if you are loud or boisterous. And it really doesn't have to do with just being mean-spirited or overly aggressive. Nope, I'm talking about something that comes from deep-down on the inside, that says *I am a woman who will be strong. I will not crumble.*

A friend of mine once received a very scary medical report about one of her children. This report could have ripped apart her marriage and devastated their family. They could have buckled under this very serious medical issue. Instead, I watched her rise up and decide what she was going to do. She and her husband had a choice to make. They had to quickly figure out what they were going to do about their child. They not only had decisions to make about her care, they also had to decide how they were going to handle it themselves. They needed to know how they were going to communicate to their family and to each other.

It's so hard on us emotionally when sudden destruction comes against us or our family. We don't get to practice how we will respond to the overwhelming fear that comes with having to deal with the possible death of a precious family member. We have no life-training to teach us how to handle that sense of despair. We need to ask ourselves the question, *how am I going to respond to this situation?* We have the opportunity right then to decide how we will deal with the feelings that come at us. Will we be consumed by fear? Will we try to get through the best we can in our own ability? Or, will we turn to God and get out our *stomping boots* as we demand the strength that God's Word promises us?

Decide Ahead of Time

We need to decide ahead of time what we will do when bad news comes our way. What's your plan of action for when you see a big old spider in the room? What happens when the doctor says you've got some kind of illness in your body? Or your husband just lost his job? In today's world, with the speed of communication, we constantly have so many issues we are dealing with. There is a never-ending supply of *bad news* and so we need to know how we are going to handle it when some of that *bad news* becomes personal.

Many people don't understand that inside strong God-thing that happens when we rise up and say, *Oh no, devil. You think just because you put that spider in the corner that you have won the battle.* And realistically, many times he does win the battle, just based on the spider being there. We can be terrified of it.

That's one reason I love the illustration of the spider in the corner. Most women quiver and shake at the sight of a spider. Honestly, spiders just give me the willies. They don't move; there is no eye contact with a spider. They don't do anything! Realistically, all they have to do is *be there,* and they win!

That is what happens with us many times. We get bad news and we totally freak out! We don't know if it is even true. We don't know that it will end in tragedy; we just immediately rush to that conclusion. That bad news (the spider in the corner) has now taken over the whole room! We let the spider dominate our thoughts. We let it make us nervous, frightened and just plain paralyzed. The tiny little spider, which could never hurt us, has taken over our emotions, our actions, and many times, our very life.

What if we don't let the spider dominate us? What if we begin by immediately getting out our stomping boots and believing God's Word when it says, *Finally my sisters, be strong in the Lord. Be strong in Him and the power of His might* (Ephesians 6:10). Instead of telling ourselves, *I can't do it, I can't do it,* why not say, *I am going to put on my stomping boots with the power of God and I am going to stomp on that situation!*

Be Strong and Very Courageous

One of my favorite verses in the Bible is found in the Old Testament book of Joshua. God told to Joshua to go take the land. God knew it would not be that easy. He knew Joshua would be afraid and nervous, so God said to him, be strong and courageous. *Then Moses called Joshua and said to him in the sight of all Israel, Be strong and of good courage, for you must go with this people to the land which the Lord has sworn to their fathers to give them; and you shall cause them to inherit it. And the Lord, He is the One who goes before you. He will be with you; He will not leave you nor forsake you; do not fear nor be dismayed* (Deuteronomy 31:7-8).

Having strength won't just happen. Strength is something that must be developed on the inside of us. We must allow it to rise up in our hearts and cause us to visualize victory, where in the natural there is none. We have been given the ability by our Father God to know that we can take the mountain; we can conquer the sickness; we can get a new job; we can repair our broken relationship.

God placed a *knowing* on the inside of each of us; a voice that tells us we just know we can conquer this situation. But, we must listen to that voice. We need to listen and respond in order to overcome the fear and doubt that is screaming in our ears. We can't cower before the *spider in the corner.* Women, more so than men, have been taught to cower. We've been taught to be afraid of everything. We've been told, *Girls don't act like that.* We've been trained to think, *I shouldn't want to be strong like that. It just isn't feminine.*

Meek Does Not Mean Weak!

Throughout history the devil has used the positive message in scripture of having a quiet and a meek spirit against women. He has twisted it into something other than what God intended. Meek does not mean weak! God didn't say you are a wonderful, godly woman if you are a trembling, mass of weakness. Meek means to be humble, not weak. A humble person is teachable, eager to learn and grow in God's ways. A teachable woman wants to be strong.

When we meet a really loud woman we may think, *Oh, that's a strong woman.* But, in reality, she is just really loud. Being loud on the outside doesn't mean a person is strong enough inside to deal with the problems that come their way. A truly strong woman has an inner strength that rises up when the occasion calls for it, and she allows God's ways to guide her steps. A strong woman knows whether the occasion calls for quietness or for something more aggressive. Sometimes, we need to be loud enough to be heard by someone who is not listening. But, we may also need to use a more quiet approach with another person. Both are based on inner strength.

Cowering can come from a past filled with devastation and hurts. Many of us, when we come to Christ, bring with us all of the pain from our past. We can't stomp on anything; *we* are the ones who have been stomped on. Many of us have had things happen to us that were not the will of God. It may have been our parents, a relative or a coach; somebody that we trusted, who stomped on us. There may have been sexual abuse, physical abuse, or even the emotional abuse of words being spoken over you for years. You may be saying, *How can I stomp on anything?* You feel like you have not recovered from being stomped on yourself.

That type of abuse really diminishes your stomping ability. That is exactly what the devil would like; for you to be forever tattooed with the inability to draw on that inner strength...the stomping kind of strength. He wants you to stay in a place of fear, cowering in a corner because of the spider in the room.

Being afraid of everything keeps you from being a person who will positively affect anyone else. You will always tell yourself, *I will never become strong enough. I can never be bold enough,* and so the devil keeps you ineffective. As a woman thinks in her heart, so is she. When we believe what those bad situations have taught us, they then gain the power in our lives to identify us.

Stomping Boot Mentality

I just want to encourage you with this thought: it takes time to develop inner strength. It is a process. You have to learn how to put on your *stomping boots,* and then learn how to walk in them. You have to learn how to speak as a person with a *stomping boot mentality.* You can, if you will take one little step – and then another step, and another; you will learn how to walk step-by-step-by-step. Please remember that this is a life-long process. We don't suddenly get from one to a hundred in ten seconds. As we walk through one situation, one issue, one problem, one-step-at-a-time we will gain strength.

Most often, when the hairy, scary spider attacks our life, our first reaction is, *Wait a minute – I think I will just let somebody else help me deal with this one.* We might think, *I'll just wait for my husband to come home and let him pray.* We want to take a pass on being the one who has to stand up and be strong. God created the marriage covenant as a partnership and within that partnership there are times we need to stomp on that spider together. The Bible clearly teaches us when two or more agree together, God is going to show up! (Matthew 19:18) We believe that and are thankful for the power of agreement.

Even though I have the best husband and he knows how to use his stomping boots, when I was diagnosed with cancer, *it wasn't in his body.* It was in my body! And it didn't matter that he wanted to stomp on that spider for me, it was still my responsibility because it was in my body. Casey did everything he could. He prayed, he believed, he stomped, he was strong, but it was still something I had to do.

Walk Strong

I had to decide I was going to kick back at the cancer in my body. I had to say, *I will be strong*. Although we work as a team and there is a wonderful agreement in our marriage relationship, we are individuals as we walk through this life. The Bible doesn't say couples are to be strong in the Lord; it says *you* be strong.

As I mentioned, agreement is great, but what happens when the person you have depended on is not there anymore? Over half the women in America aren't currently married. Many women don't have a husband who will come alongside them and be strong. Many of us don't have family or friends close by who will stand on the Word of God with us when something attacks our lives.

We all recognize that life is full of incidences and – whether you are married or not, have a strong support system or not – every individual must meet our own challenges. We all must endure the tests and trials of life. We all come under attack of the devil, because the devil comes to steal, to kill and to destroy. But, the good news is, Jesus came to give us the strength and power we need to overcome the attacks of the enemy (John 10:10).

One of the most common ways the devil comes against women is in our emotions. I can feel bad about myself and say to Casey, *Oh I just feel bad. I feel bad about this...and I feel bad about that.* He can pray for me, encourage me and even speak the Word over me, but guess what? He may have prayed for me, but I will still feel bad if I haven't gotten the spider out of my corner. I forgot to open the door, turn on the lights and STOMP!

There is something about stomping for yourself that says, *I refuse to let the spider win!* I have to take what God has for me individually. I have to apply the Word myself and let God's powerful life flow out of me. Do not become disheartened or discouraged, and don't allow yourself to compare your ability with anyone else's. We are not in a competition; we are all in our own race of growing and developing and learning how to wear our stomping boots. Do what you can do today. If you do what you can do today, then you will be able to do what you need to do tomorrow.

The First Step

The first step to developing that *stomping attitude* is simply saying, *I will.* Once you say *I'm going to,* you have taken a giant leap. The first step is always the hardest step. But it is also the most meaningful. You aren't going anywhere without that first step!

Casey and I went on a new adventure not too long ago. We did a zip line challenge course and it included walking across a high wire! At over 50 feet off the ground! Now, I didn't have to do it. Nobody made me. I actually volunteered to do it. In fact, I paid to do it! But, I have to tell you that first step was tough! That one step can almost take your breath away...it's what I call the "ha" step. You know, if you can only take that one step, you will be on your way! Once I took that first step onto the wire, the next step was easier. The next steps that followed were even easier, because I was already doing it.

That first step puts you on the path to success. It puts you on the pathway of saying, *No devil, you don't get to win.* At that point, you know you will do all it takes to walk into your victory! When I was working to get across that high wire I didn't care if it took me one baby step, by baby step, by baby step, by baby step. In fact, I did take a lot of those tiny little baby steps! But, I made it to the other side, and no one cared how long it took me or how many steps I needed...all that mattered was that I made it!

Please realize that we will *all* be taking those baby steps from now until we leave this earth. If all we can do is take a baby step every day, guess what? Those baby steps, which we are taking from now until we get to heaven will take us the distance, and we will have gotten the victory. That is all we're asked to do.

The Next Step

In the natural world, what happens after you stomp on that big old spider? Oh yeah, you freak out! Freaking out is absolutely what we all do! Let's just all agree, squishing a spider is creepy! There isn't anyone who feels they can do it without hesitation or doubt. It's not possible. We all have the thought, *Somebody else could do this. Somebody else is stronger than me. Somebody else is better than me. Somebody else is more spiritual than me.*

I have been saved for over 30 years and I still have those thoughts. Even now I can think, *Somebody else can do this better or be stronger. Somebody else would be better than me.* But, I have also come to the place where I say to myself, *Yeah, I have that thought. So what? Am I going to walk away from the calling of God? Walk away from what He has placed before me, just because I am fearful or tired?* I refuse to let the thought that I cannot take the next step stop me. I refuse to say, *I will not take the step.* Sure, I'm afraid. I'm feeling like I'm not sure I can do it. I'm not sure of the results. But, I will not bow down to that feeling or that thought.

Sometimes as we take the next step, we feel like we just stepped in a mud puddle. It feels all gushy and wet and nasty. We are thinking, *What was that?* We thought we were taking a good step and suddenly, whoop! We are in the middle of a mess. Okay – we stepped in a mud puddle – but it doesn't mean God turned away from us. He doesn't say, with great disappointment, *I can't believe my daughter just stepped in that mud puddle. I'm just going to ignore her now and not love her anymore.*

Many of us have a wrong view of God and how our relationship with Him works. We have thought that He is constantly an *on again, off again* God. He will love me – He won't love me. He loves me – He doesn't love me. We have this kind of *daisy mentality* – He loves me, He loves me not, loves me, loves me not, loves me, loves me not. We are constantly picking petals to decide how we think God feels about us. No! We must stomp on that kind of thinking! God doesn't play the picking petals game of, *I love you, I love you not.* He has already chosen you! He has written in His Word, *I love you, forever.*

His Love Never Changes

Even when we don't experience victory, it doesn't change His love for us. Nothing changes His love. We can live all of our lives on earth and have no victory whatsoever, and it will not change God's loves for us. If we are born again, we will walk into heaven and be accepted whether or not we were victorious over the battles we faced on earth. The only thing that can separate us from God is our salvation; whether or not we choose to accept Jesus as our Lord and Savior. In the end, nothing else really matters.

Living on earth without winning our battles might not feel good, and we might not get the rewards (because the Bible teaches us there are rewards), but that doesn't change His love for us. I pray that, as believers, we get a revelation of God's love for us. If we truly understood how much He loves us and how our works on earth don't affect that, it would be life-changing. The devil would not be able to come and spin his webs all around us. He would be limited in the way he could weave into the different affairs of our life. From relationships to finances, to our children's lives; he would be stopped from bringing in deception, lies and problems.

Think of it like this: the devil is the spider, and he is spinning his webs around us. As the webs begin to entangle us, we need to ask, *Am I going to let that web stay?* We often choose to let the web stay. Or we can stomp out the web, attacking it until we get to the place of victory. It becomes our choice...let the webs stay and continue to grow, or get rid of them! It really comes down to our willingness to say, *I'm putting these stomping boots on and I'm going to stomp!* We have to let that kind of spirit rise up inside of us, take those baby steps and keep going.

Being Planted in the Church

In fighting the battles of life, I have to mention the extreme value that comes from being planted in a local church. Remember, we talked about having people in your life to count on when the trials of life come your way.

Who do you have in your life that will stand with you when you are covered in spider webs? Being a committed part of the family of God, a.k.a. your local church, you become linked with others who believe as you do. These are the ones who will encourage and build you up when you are trying to fight through the difficulties that come your way.

The Bible teaches that the New Testament churches were founded on the fellowship of the saints. They gathered weekly to encourage, help, and build each other up. They helped in time of need, prayed together and worshipped the Lord. That is what should be happening in our local churches today. Unfortunately, many of us have been in churches where nobody really knows us. We come and go and no one really knows or cares...or so it seems. In many cases, we have become a society of individuals rather than a community of people who love, help and applaud each other.

One of the major life-decisions you should make is what kind of church you will attend. Personally, I am going to be in a church where we applaud each other, and encourage each other. (A side note: Remember, church isn't full of perfect people. Sometimes people will mess up and won't always do everything just right. Remind yourself, you don't do everything right all the time either, so don't judge others more harshly than you would want to be judged.)

As Christians, it is to our benefit to regularly spend time gathering together, listening to the Word, and building relationships with one another. As we are planted in the house of God, with deep roots from years of serving, giving and building relationships, we will have strength when problems come our way.

Don't Isolate Yourself

Sadly, too many Christians operate with a very independent attitude; they keep themselves isolated. This may be due to feeling the need to hide certain aspects of our lives. We may not want anyone to know we've actually got to *stomp* on something. We may have financial difficulties or have lost our job. I've known people who waited months before they told anyone that they lost their job. I always wonder why. I think it could be because their ego has gotten in the way. We can all feel challenged to share our struggles, but our ego can also stop us from experiencing the victory God has for us.

What does your ego really matter when you think of the scope of your whole life? Why hide everything? It's easy to hide, but why not have the people around you be a part of your victory? Why not ask them to stomp that devil with you? With two of you in agreement, boom! You've got strength! You've got your victory.

I love the example of the *spider in the corner* because it is such a great visual. If there is one thing we all know, it's that *spiders just show up*. They show up out of nowhere. You can clean out all the little crevices around your house and think you are good, when suddenly you have a spider in your house again. The devil is like that too!

Remember, the devil comes to try and destroy your life. And guess what? He doesn't just go away. We don't get to stomp him one time and have him disappear from our lives forever. We would all like to stomp him once and never have to stomp him again. Just like the spiders in our house don't leave forever, the devil also comes back over and over to wreak havoc in our lives.

It's natural to think that once we have dealt with the spider it will never come back. It's funny how amazed we are to see them pop back up. It's the same with God. We pray, believe we receive, and even see the results; but when something bad comes into our lives we are shocked! We say, God, *where are You?* We question where God is, not fully understanding what it means when we say, *WE LIVE ON THE EARTH!*

We think because we had the exterminators come and spray everything that those spiders are gone forever. We stomped all the spiders and they are out of our house. Then, suddenly, six months later here come a bunch of new spiders all over again. A whole new crop of problems just showed up! We live on a cursed earth, and we need to realize we will never, *not* have spiders. We will never, not have the devil coming against us in our lives. We will never ever, *not* find a spider in the corner. Those spiders are here to stay and so is the devil. He will keep popping up in our lives, because it is his job to destroy us.

The Devil Is Not Nice!

We have a kind of *story book* view of the devil. We have seen him pictured over and over as a little red devil with little horns. We think he isn't really all that bad or scary. We have to wake up and get a true picture of who he really is. He is wicked, bad, ugly, and full of deceit. He wants to kill you! He wants to destroy your life. He wants to steal your joy, steal your peace, and steal your finances. He wants to steal your relationships and your health. He is every bit of wickedness you can imagine. There is *nothing* good in him.

That is why we cannot allow ourselves to be disheartened when there is something going on in our lives. We can't sit back and say, *I'm just so tired*

– *devil, get out of here.* Really? You think that is going to make him run? Do you look at the spider in your house, and say in a whiney voice, *Go away, spider. I don't like you. Just go away!* Do you really think that spider is going anywhere? Personally, I don't think spiders are real intelligent, but there aren't any spiders I've ever seen who would take off after being talked to like that. No, if the spider could talk, he would say, *Are you kidding me? Yeah, time to keep spinning my web. I'm going to stay right here.*

We have all seen spiders take off running when we try to grab them. When they see us coming, they try to run off and hide. That's why we need our stomping boots! Our life is full of *stomping boots moments.* We may put on many different shoes throughout the day for various reasons, but we never get rid of our stomping boots.

As long as we are on earth, our stomping boots will be a part of our lives. We will wear them until the day we walk into Heaven. So we need to learn how to best wear our stomping boots right now.

Take Time to Rejoice

Another very important aspect of wearing our stomping boots is this: Take time to rejoice! Remember the story of how I had to use my stomping boots to overcome cancer in my body? I had to go through a process to get to the victory. I had to go through the surgery; then, I had to figure out what to do during the initial recovery time; finally, I had to get help to figure out the different kinds of medications I needed to take. Sometimes, in the midst of all of the details, we can forget to rejoice and thank God for what He has done.

Did I have the victory? Absolutely!! Even though I had things I still needed to do, I also needed to take time to rejoice. I needed that special moment to say, *Yes! This is so cool! God, You are so good. Thank You!* We sometimes rush past the part where we honor God for what He has done!

When we read through the Book of Psalms, we realize David was constantly honoring and praising God for all the things He had done. He was very poetic about how much he loved God and he really expressed his gratitude. I love how many times in the Old Testament they would build an altar. I know we don't do that today, but I love how they took the time to really make note of what God had done. We don't really do that in our culture. We act more like, *Oh yeah, by the way, thanks!*

Don't Grow Weary

The other thing we see as we read through Psalms is this: although David often expressed his gratitude, just as often he said, *Hey, God, I need some help.* Sometimes there are problems and sometimes there is victory. Our life, as believers, is full victory, but we will also always have problems. If we aren't aware, this is where we can become very disheartened. It can feel like, *Sure, I just experienced the victory, but as soon as I turn around I've got another problem.* That is one of the most challenging realities of earth-life. We need to acknowledge that. We need to accept the fact that earth life is not heaven. That is why earth-life comes with *stomping boots.* And, when we get victory, we rejoice in those victories.

I rejoiced when I had victory over cancer. But, the next day I had to put on my stomping boots to figure out the right medication to take so my body would work correctly. Victory was for a moment, but then it was time to get back to work. It would have been easy to be discouraged and say, *Man, I had to go through the surgery and lost part of my body. Now I have to figure out what to do with the medication. Why God? What did I do wrong?* I could have been mad about what happened, or I could say, *Thank You, God, that this cancer was detected in time.* I had the choice to say; *Thank God, the cancer is gone now.* I had the choice to be mad or thank God for a good doctor and that the medicine I needed was available.

Is it easy? No, it's not easy all the time. Life doesn't come with a guarantee to be perfect and easy. But, we do have a guarantee in God's Word that He will never leave us or forsake us. He will never leave us without an answer or without hope. He knows what we are going through and He gave us *stomping boots* to help us win! Those little spiders will try and crawl out of the woodwork because they want to kill, steal and destroy. But we, as women of God, have an inner strength that won't let us down. We have amazing perseverance. We have this thing that God puts within the hearts of us women; *we are warriors.*

Warrior women, let's rise up. Rise up and put on your *stomping boots!* Do not allow yourself to grow weary. Run and don't faint! Just remember, it is not about *your* strength. It is about the strength of Almighty God working within you every moment of every day.

For additional tools, tips, and training, go to shoeswisely.org

CHAPTER FOUR

Toe to Toe, Heel to Heal

Toe to Toe, Heel to Heal

Every girl needs a pair of boxing shoes! Boxing is a combat sport and as Christians, there are times when we must lace up our boxing shoes to fight our enemy, the devil. Let me warn you, like everything else in the Kingdom of God, God's ways oppose the world's way. To the world, boxing shoes represent fighting. As Christians, what do our boxing shoes represent? They represent forgiveness.

When we think of forgiveness, we don't think of combat. We think of gentleness, and kindness and mercy. Forgiveness is a powerful and necessary weapon in fighting the enemy because without it, the devil has the upper hand. No boxer ever wants to give his opponent the upper hand.

What do you know about boxing? I personally don't know much, but when I think of boxing, I think of the weight classes. A boxer can be a featherweight, a lightweight, a welterweight or a heavyweight just to name a few; however, to be strong in their sport, every boxer has to be lean and quick. The boxing legend Muhammad Ali coined the phrase, *Float like a butterfly, sting like a bee*. Well, to float like a butterfly, we must be pretty light on our feet!

Let Go of the Weight

The Scripture says in Hebrews 12:1, *Therefore we also, since we are surrounded by so great a cloud of witnesses, let us lay aside every weight, and the sin which so easily ensnares us, and let us run with endurance the race that is set before us...* When we hear...*let us lay aside every weight,* what do we visualize? I think of the weight unforgiveness brings to our emotions and our soul. A person dealing with unforgiveness spends a great deal of energy pondering what caused their pain. Their spiritual eyes are unfocused. Their spiritual reflexes are dull; anger, frustration, and a sense of inadequacy rule their life. No doubt about it, unforgiveness will weigh us down and create heaviness in our lives.

Lace Up Those Shoes

Just as professional boxers put on their boxing shoes, we need to put on our shoes to be lean, flexible and ready to work. In boxing, we've got to jab, to move, and to work out enough to sweat. Our *boxing shoes* help us do that, but they are not all that easy and simple to put on our feet. It takes effort to tie those tall laces. Unlike our dressy slip-on shoes or our flip flops, boxing shoes take time. We've got to work our foot into them, pull the tongue up, tighten the strings from the bottom to the top, adjust the tongue, in some cases, loop the laces around the hooks and tie them. Some boxers also wrap the laces around the top of the shoe a couple of times before tying them.

Likewise, forgiveness takes effort, and must be done intentionally. Forgiveness is an on purpose, well-thought-out, unemotional decision. Now somebody reading this could say, *Yeah, right! My father sexually abused me. My neighbor molested me. I was raped. My father beat me. My husband cheated on me. I lost a child.*

Forgive the Unforgivable

You know, I get it. I understand why you may be angry, and why you want to stay angry. Something *unforgivable* was done to you. It was unfair, and you could be angry and unforgiving about that situation all of your life. On top of that, most people would agree with you and say, *Yes, you have a right to be angry!* Betrayal is all around us. Abandonment is all around us. Just sit down in a room full of women and say, *Hey, what happened to you?* And the conversation could quickly turn into a competition of sharing life's worst stories. We all have stories whether we were raised in very safe environments or not.

I was raised in a very safe environment. My parents didn't abuse me. My siblings didn't beat me or sexually molest me. Yet, even in my innocent and protected life, I have absolutely felt abandoned in relationships. I have felt betrayal from friends; people who had said yes, but their actions said no. In fact, I would like to share one particular life-changing event that, as a young girl, had a significant effect on me.

Growing up, I was a pastor's kid, and I loved it. I remember always being happy. My dad was a denominational pastor, and we always lived right next to the church. I loved being at the church, and would often wander over during my free time just to play and hang out.

One night, as I ran over to the church, I noticed they were having a meeting. There were probably 100 people there, and I knew every one of them. I thought to myself, *these are all my friends – my church family*. I talked and visited with them, and walked home only to find out that they were actually meeting to vote my father out as pastor. They did not like his teaching, so they moved him out. Well, that meant I had to also move. In my heart, these great Christian people had just betrayed me!

This was a devastating time for my family. My dad went into a very deep depression. He also felt alone and betrayed. My parents' marriage went through turmoil, and my siblings and I also were challenged with all the changes in our family. The incident not only disrupted our family's life, but it caused many other problems.

We Have a Choice

Now, I had to make a choice: I could walk down the horrible road of feeling betrayed and abandoned every time I remembered this story, or I could make a decision to forgive those feelings of betrayal and sadness, and then settle it in my heart. It says in John 20:23, *If you forgive the sins of any, they are forgiven them; if you retain the sins of any, they are retained.* Sin will cling to you. Unforgiveness will bind you. Retaining sin and unforgiveness are like putting chains around your body and trying to walk. It's just impossible to move with that heaviness all around you. We can't be light on our feet when we allow sin to bind us.

In my circumstance, I had a choice. I could live with a spirit of unforgiveness because of the effect the church's decision had on my family.

Instead of my *boxing shoes,* I could have put on my kick-them-in-the-behind boots and given them a swift kick! And guess what? The world would agree with me; they would encourage me to live in unforgiveness and take the easy way out!

But unforgiveness and anger won't set us free. The kicking boots are easier to put on than boxing shoes, but that does not mean they are the right shoe to wear. Unforgiveness is like a magnet; as we allow the weight of unforgiveness to attach itself to us, we become bonded to the pain. The Bible clearly teaches we have retained that sin.

As we put on our boxing shoes and tie those babies up, we are intentionally deciding to lay aside the weight that can easily overthrow us. We have chosen to live in forgiveness because the Word teaches that when we forgive others, we allow God to forgive us. *For if you forgive men their trespasses, your heavenly father will also forgive you* (Matthew 6:14). If we want the fullness of God's forgiveness in our lives, we must fully forgive others. It is impossible to live the fullness of life without having forgiveness in our hearts.

Take Time to Forgive

When I first became a Christian and learned about forgiveness, I remember one of my teachers saying, *Take time to really forgive those in your life who may have hurt you in the past.* In other words, take the time on purpose to go back through your life, walk through it in your heart and mind to give and receive forgiveness. As a result, during my time of prayer, I asked the Holy Spirit to help me walk down the road of forgiveness. God says in John 14 that the Holy Spirit is our Comforter and our Helper. *If you love Me, you will keep My commandments. And I will pray the Father, and He will give you another Helper, that He may abide with you forever—the Spirit of Truth, Whom the world cannot receive, because it neither sees Him or knows Him, for He dwells with you and will be in you* (John 14:15-17).

You and I cannot forgive just because we want to do it. We can assume we will just do it, but our minds and our emotions will take us right back to the pain. Our flesh resists forgiveness. We cannot forgive in and of our own will; which is why we have been given the help of our Comforter, the Holy Spirit. God's Word teaches us in 1 John 4 that greater is God who lives in us than he that is in the world. *You are of God, little children, and have overcome them, because He who is in you is greater than he who is in the world* (1 John 4:4).

We have God living in us. We do not need to try to depend upon our natural ability to forgive. We can ask, *God, help me to have Your spirit of forgiveness because You love me. Father God, help me to forgive those who have hurt me! Holy Spirit, You are my Comforter. Help me to let go of this heavy weight I am carrying!*

Once I learned of my need to forgive those in my past, my morning prayer time became a place of healing and freedom. I asked God to walk with me through my history. I asked Him to help me get rid of those weights that had been keeping me down. I started at the top of my list at that time, with my family. I began with my dad first, then my mom, and finally I went through each of my siblings (I have five siblings).

During my intimate prayer time each day I opened myself up and talked to the Holy Spirit about them. I asked, *God is there anything about my relationship with my dad that I need to forgive? Is there anything I need to ask forgiveness for?* If there were thoughts or incidents that came to mind about my dad, I addressed them with God. Maybe your dad said hurtful words or had actions that negatively affected you. You can do this same thing. It is a relatively simple process to spend time talking to God and really making sure your heart is clean.

Next, God and I talked about my mom, and then my siblings. Some of these took longer than others, and I did not try to make this a one-day event. I made sure that I had time to cover everyone in a way that felt complete to me. I was able to address everyone in a short period of time – perhaps a week. I then went on to address other people who had been significant in my life, such as teachers who may have influenced me; plus different girls who had been my close friends and a few boyfriends.

The Holy Spirit Walks Us Through

During this time of putting on our *boxing shoes,* the Holy Spirit will walk with us through different parts of our past, and at times, we will feel different emotions. In my case, sometimes I felt sad, but I always asked the Holy Spirit in that time of sadness to help me release the weight of unforgiveness. I often prayed, *Father God, help me release the weight of feeling left out, betrayed or like someone just broke my trust.*

I have friends who have dealt with much more difficult situations in their past than I have had to deal with. As I mentioned, my childhood did not include any type of abuse or really serious problems. But my friends have had to conquer the weight of emotional, physical, and sexual abuse. And still, they have decided to trust the Holy Spirit and say, *I choose to forgive.*

Those are big words. I really believe some of the most powerful words we can speak are, *I choose to forgive.* Will we feel free the first time we say those words? No, probably not. But, we still must chose forgiveness over the weight and heaviness of our pain.

Another thought my friends shared with me was the importance of daily speaking their forgiveness. Every day they would say, *Father God, I am choosing forgiveness.* Some situations have caused deeper pain than others and will take more time to heal. Some situations are more quickly resolved because the hurt was not as deep. But if the thought continued to come up, they would say again, *I'm letting go of that weight. I am choosing forgiveness. As the book of John teaches, I'm not going to retain that sin.* They daily put on their boxing shoes and chose to live in forgiveness.

One friend has a great testimony of how putting on her *boxing shoes* worked for her. She said at first, she would remember and feel the pain every single day. Then it became every other day, and eventually, it became every week. Finally, it became every month until it got to a place that when she began to speak with the Father God about that situation, she realized that as she had made the choice to forgive, freedom came. She was released from the pain of that horrible situation.

Sometimes We Still Have Scars

Some people say, *Forgive and forget.* I honestly don't believe you forget. I just don't believe that. I think that we have a brilliant mind which remembers and recalls vividly the incidents that have happened in our lives. Those incidents leave scars. While the pain may be gone, and we have been healed, the scar remains.

To this day, I have a scar on my leg from an accident that occurred when I was going into the sixth grade. I was hit by a car and almost died. After being healed, the accident left a big scar on my left leg. As with our physical body, our emotional history has often left scars. I can feel and touch the scar with my hand, but I feel no pain. The scar is still there – but it no longer causes me any pain.

We all have scars, whether they are physical or emotional. Something hit us. Someone violated us, but now the pain is gone. We will probably not forget the incident, and actually, I don't know how wise it is to forget. Sometimes our scars can bring healing to other people. We have walked through trials and tribulations, and as we conquer those issues through forgiveness, we can speak of those moments without pain, and genuinely share what happened in our lives to benefit others.

The Journey Toward Healing

While some of us may have already dealt with our past and some are still on their journey toward healing, we all need to approach today with our boxing shoes laced up and ready to let go of offenses. Every day we must choose to forgive; we must choose to let go of hurt. Things will happen in our day – someone might forget our birthday, our husband does something, our children talk wrong, our friend doesn't call when she said she would, or we get fired from our job when we shouldn't have. We must keep our boxing shoes on for the big stuff and the small stuff. We are fighting the fight of faith.

As powerful women of God, let's live in freedom and refuse to let unforgiveness weigh us down. In order to stay light on our feet, we daily decide, *before an incident happens,* to forgive. We've already determined to forgive when something happens; we are already wearing our boxing shoes. We have already chosen forgiveness! We believe the reality of God's Word, so no matter what happens in our day, in our week, and in our years to come, we forgive.

While You Are Forgiving Others, Others Are Forgiving You

God so loved us that He forgave us when we offended Him with sin. Why would we think we haven't offended others here on Earth as well, and sinned against them? Remember, while you are forgiving others, others are forgiving you. No one has walked through life perfectly. We cannot walk this earth thinking we have never stepped on someone's toes, betrayed someone, said something inappropriate or acted wrong. I love how the Message Bible says it in Luke 6:37-38

> *Don't pick on people, jump on their failures, criticize their faults—unless, of course, you want the same treatment. Don't condemn those who are down; that hardness can boomerang. Be easy on people; you'll find life a lot easier. Give away your life; you'll find life given back, but not merely given back—given back with bonus and blessing. Giving, not getting is the way. Generosity begets generosity.*

It goes both ways; we have hurt others and others have hurt us. We didn't mean to do that. Well, perhaps we did at times because we are so human and fleshly. We have all done something inappropriate at times, but ask for forgiveness and freely give forgiveness. Let's put on our boxing shoes and live with a light and free spirit of forgiveness.

> *Therefore we also, since we are surrounded by so great a cloud of witnesses, let us lay aside every weight, and the sin which so easily ensnares us, and let us run with endurance the race that is set before us, looking unto Jesus, the author and finisher of our faith, who for the joy that was set before Him endured the cross, despising the shame, and has sat down at the right hand of the throne of God* (Hebrews 12:1-3).

Our Boxing Shoes Are Light

Boxing shoes are lightweight, soft and pliable. They are made to allow us to freely move around life's boxing ring. Inevitably, we all have to fight our adversary in the ring, but we can win our battles if we don't have sin and unforgiveness weighing us down. If professional boxers went into the boxing ring with big weights on their feet, they couldn't move. They couldn't get out of the way or jump in to deliver a winning punch. They wouldn't be able to accomplish very much. That is exactly what happens when we carry unforgiveness. Unforgiveness puts weight on us, affecting our feet, our steps, and our ability to move. We are weighed down instead of being light on our feet.

When unforgiveness is working in you, there's no bounce in your step. That bounce represents joy and a spirit of life, as opposed to a person who is holding on to the weights and challenges. Those weights will get heavier if left unaddressed. But the Spirit of God wants to lift us so that we have bounce in our step instead of heaviness.

Perhaps some may still want to say, *You don't understand what happened to me! How can I forgive?* I will not even attempt to say I understand. I don't. But you can rely on the fact that God does. You could say, *Yeah, then why didn't God stop it?* My friend, God is all love. Because of His love, He has given mankind free choice and free will. With that will, people have done things that are totally contrary to our loving Father God.

Our Father would never, ever bring evil to any of His kids. God did not plan that hurt nor was He a part of the bad things done to you. Instead, His gift is the ability to live free from that pain. The devil is always the one who comes to steal, kill and destroy. *The thief does not come except to steal, and to kill, and to destroy. I have come that they may have life, and that they may have it more abundantly* (John 10:10).

The devil comes to destroy your future and keep you bound with those weights. He wants to knock you out in the ring, so you have to decide. Let God's love help you. Believe that He has only come to give you abundant life. He wants to give you hope that your future is bright. He wants to bring total victory out of the destruction that has held you down.

How do we live a life of total victory? We first forgive; and then we remain ready with our *boxing shoes* on. We keep our hearts open and ready to forgive at all times. We rely on God, who knows all about our pain, to help us. We understand that God was not the author of our pain.

Staying Free!

Have you ever found yourself rehearsing your past pain? By that I mean, we let our minds dwell on the past. We let thoughts creep back in, and we find ourselves immersed in those feelings all over again. We may think, *Wow! I thought I had already forgiven that person.* Remember, our memories are still a part of us. We don't get to erase it from our memory banks forever. We are just feeling the scar. When that happens we have to remind ourselves, *No! That is just a scar. I've dealt with it, and it's all done. It is over because I am choosing to walk in the love of God, and in forgiveness.*

Let me end with one last component of our boxing shoes. Although forgiveness is our choice, it does not mean that we need to have a relationship with the person who hurt us. It does not mean we will regularly talk with them or hang out with them. A relationship like that takes trust, and trust is an earned commodity.

When something has happened to us on a level where we need to forgive someone, it often breaks our trust. Trust may or may not be rebuilt. We may or may not maintain the relationship. We have to pray and seek God about the wisdom of allowing that person back into our lives. The spirit of forgiveness is about freeing us and our heart so that we are not tattooed by and bound to our past. It does not necessarily free that person. It frees us.

What if They Never Ask for Forgiveness?

What if a person who hurt us continues to blame us for what happened? What about the person who uses sneaky, dominating ways of bringing it all back up, making us feel we are wrong? I would say more often than not, people are not going to ask us to forgive them. They will not come to us and say, *I did you wrong.*

Please remember: Forgiveness is not about the other person. Forgiveness is about us! We are making a choice for our own soul. Like the people who were kicking my dad out of the church; not one of them has ever tracked me down and said, *By the way, how are you? I realize that what happened could have really damaged you and I'm sorry for that.* As far as I know, not one of them has considered how their actions may have affected me and my family. I had to make the choice to forgive for the peace of my own soul, regardless of what they did.

I could go down the list of situations where people have abandoned me, and I have felt hurt. I can say very, very few people have ever come to me to ask for forgiveness. Although that is probably true for most of us, we can't base forgiveness on what a person does for us. We base our forgiveness on what Jesus did for us and our personal desire to be free!

Our *boxing shoes* are lightweight with soft soles. We can even dance around our enemy in them because we are not weighed down with unforgiveness. They protect our feet, and at the same time keep us light and free. To be properly prepared to fight our enemy, we've got to put on our boxing shoes. Our *boxing shoes* of forgiveness are necessary to effectively fight – let's fight to win!

For additional tools, tips, and training, go to shoeswisely.org

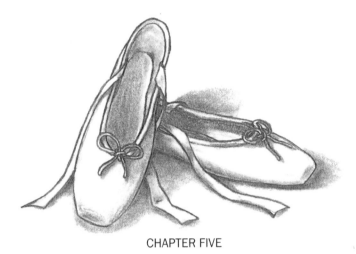

CHAPTER FIVE

Cut Loose, Foot Loose

Cut Loose, Foot Loose

Visualize a little girl in her sweet little princess dress as she twirls and twirls. Every little girl, when she puts on her princess dress just has to twirl and say, *Look at me, look at me!* She is dancing with joy! And her joy is contagious!

My Tasha has always twirled and danced. She was that kind of little girl; one who exuded joy and life. To me, watching her has always been a perfect example of the spirit of joy in life. That same spirit of joy communicates the essence of our dancing shoes. The happy, exuberant, without restraint...pure joy of life *dancing shoes!*

In life there are moments when we need to put on our dancing shoes to get us through situations. But, there are also many occasions we get to on purpose put on our dancing shoes to celebrate. There are those special moments, like a wedding dance, where we get to celebrate something magnificent in our lives.

Moments of Unbelievable Joy

When I watched my daughter, as she danced with her new husband, Moses, at their wedding, her face reflected this unbelievable joy. Seeing her face was the *gold of life* for me. It was the precious, one-of-a-kind moment that doesn't happen often in our lives. Her joy radiated from her, and to witness that was so amazing. We need to take those moments and savor them. Many times we forget how important it is to put on that spirit of joy...to put on our *dancing shoes.*

It just makes me smile when I think of putting dancing shoes onto the warrior woman, who was earlier wearing her stomping boots. But, that's what we do! In the space of one day, we can change our shoes so many times. We go from prayer feet, to stomping boots, to dancing shoes all in one day. I love the ability God has given us to move from moment to moment...to change from one way of doing something to the next as the need arises.

All of the different shoes that we wear in life are necessary. They are good and they are important, but we cannot forget to put on our dancing shoes throughout the day, because the joy of the Lord is our strength – and, *a merry heart does good, like medicine, but a broken spirit dries the bones* (Proverbs 17:22). We are also told in Nehemiah: *Then he said to them, Go your way, eat the fat, drink the sweet, and send portions to those for whom nothing is prepared; for this day is holy to our Lord. Do not sorrow, for the joy of the LORD is your strength* (Nehemiah 8:10).

Healing Comes Through Joy

God is saying something important through these scriptures: there is healing that is brought through joy. He is also teaching us this: if you are sad and broken in your spirit, it dries up your bones. I honestly believe many people get sick and die young because they have not put on their dancing shoes. They have not allowed joy to surround them in those times when they really needed it. We seriously need the joy, the laughter, the merriness, the exuberance that comes when we put on our *dancing shoes*.

When Casey was diagnosed with hepatitis C and was on chemotherapy for eleven months, one of the things we recognized right away was that we were going to need joy in our lives. From the very beginning of his chemotherapy treatments we made a plan. We knew going in that this would be a long, tough battle.

It is unbelievably hard to go through the process of chemotherapy. Many times the side effects of these drugs are worse than the disease you are trying to heal. You can't eat, you don't sleep well. It wreaks havoc with your emotions. Some of you know what I'm talking about. You have lived with people or you yourself have gone through chemotherapy for cancer or hepatitis C or some kind of horrible disease that just leeches the life out of you.

Get Your Battle Plan Ready

Casey and I decided, as he walked into this battle, we were going to have to do something different if we were going to make it through. We approached this battle as a team. As a team, we planned what we were going to do on a daily basis. When you walk into this kind of battle, you cannot just have a vague idea that you will win, and not know exactly how you plan to win. We knew we would have to demand certain things of ourselves in order to keep going when things got really tough.

One thing we decided on was to keep joy as a part of our daily lives. We knew if we got down and depressed we would not win. We not only decided to have joy, we were very detailed with how we would make that happen. It's much harder to get our battle plan ready when we are already in the middle of it! We were in agreement to demand of ourselves to have joy in our home. We demanded of ourselves to bring in a spirit of laughter...and it wasn't always easy! We didn't always have the natural ability to just sit there and laugh. It's hard to smile, let alone laugh, especially when we are hurting.

One way we brought laughter into our home was by getting videos of some of those old-time, funny comedians. We found some of the old-fashioned, clean comedy that was pure entertainment from years ago. There are many comedians today who are just sarcastic and mean towards people. That is not the type of humor I am talking about. There is no true joy when we ridicule other people. Obviously many people like that style of humor, but does it really benefit us in our soul to be a part of that mean spirit? Why put that into our heart and mind when there are comics who have done some truly hilarious things that don't mock or hurt anyone.

There is one situation I remember so clearly: As I walked into our home one day, I heard Casey upstairs just laughing. I could hear his laughter throughout the house. Knowing how extremely sick he was - he was not eating anything and barely sleeping a few hours a night – it just made me laugh, hearing him laugh. It made me feel like I had my husband back, even if it was only for a few moments. It made me want to do that joy-filled dance of life. The twirling, laughing, joyous dance!

Don't Jump in the Mud

It is so important to keep that spirit of joy; the dancing, laughing, joy in our lives. When we are in horrible, horrible moments our natural inclination is to jump into the mud and roll around in it. Not everyone will jump right into depression but some of us, more so than others, really need to have our battle plan ready for when those times come.

Some people have a natural tendency to lean towards the darker side of life. In my past, I have been the type of person who has leaned toward depression, the darker side of life. My dad was very depressed as I was growing up, so I lived with that spirit of depression in my home. It was very familiar and comfortable to me. For many of us, it is very comfortable to embrace the problems of life; we really *feel* the problem and we love to tell people about the problem.

Embracing our problems will never cause us to have victory. In fact, the Bible says, living like that *dries out our bones!* What does it mean to have dried out bones? We live life without any joy! The merriness, laughter, and joy of life is eliminated from us, and instead we live with sadness, emptiness, a sense of dullness and that gives place for sickness to come into our life.

Embrace God's Word

When I heard Casey laughing that day, I felt the presence of the Word of God in our midst. Sadness and pain or joy and healing; both have a presence in our life. We choose which one to embrace by either living according to our own ways, or by acting on God's Word. When we obey God's Word we reap the results of His Word and we bring His presence into our lives. Instead of defeat, victory is released.

Casey and I have chosen to release joy by putting on our dancing shoes daily. It is a daily *on purpose* choice, because in life we all have our own issues at times. Not all the time. Every single day is not going to bring an overwhelming problem we have to deal with. But sometimes just living life can actually suck the life right out of us. Just living life – with all the different stresses we have to deal with as women – we have to, on purpose, put on our *dancing shoes.*

So what can we do to *on purpose* put on our *dancing shoes?* Different people do that different ways. Tasha, our daughter, will literally get up and just dance. She will just get up and dance around the room! But my daughter-in-law, Christa, will sing; which is just hysterical, because she cannot sing. She doesn't walk into my house without singing; we hear her coming in the door, singing totally off key, loud as can be! And she brings with her that spirit of joy; that dancing spirit!

Everybody laughs when Christa sings, because she knows she can't sing, and she does it anyway! She carries with her a spirit of joy. That is what I am talking about; how can we put on our *dancing shoes* and embrace that spirit of joy and laughter in our life. How can we remind ourselves daily that not everything *has to be so serious* all the time!

No Excuses

If you have a more somber personality you may need to learn from somebody with the joyful qualities you desire to have. Don't resent people who act happier than you. Don't give yourself the excuse, *Well, if they had to live my life they wouldn't be so happy.* It is easy to be resentful and push away the very thing that would help you. Don't push away the people who look at life a little bit lighter, because in the long run it is smarter to start seeing life through their eyes; health comes through a merry heart.

Health comes from participating in the *dance of life.* It comes from not being so serious about every situation that comes at us in a day. Even in the midst of a hellish situation, we have to learn how to put on our dancing shoes. Put on the shoes that demands of us to laugh or get around somebody who has a spirit of joyfulness in their life and let them share that joy with you.

One of the great values of being part of a local church is having relationships with people who will lift you up. I don't know how people survive without having strong, long-term Christian friends to pray with, talk with, and laugh with when times get hard. Friends who are walking the same direction and will stand with us bring great joy into our lives.

Laugh For No Reason

Not too long ago, one of my friends and I were talking about joy, and I said, *I don't know - I can't imagine that people just laugh for no reason.* She called across the room to her husband and said, *hey, just laugh!* And he just started to laugh. It was so hilarious! They were both trained actors, so they had done this kind of thing before. But, it was amazing to watch...as he started to laugh, his wife started to laugh. Soon every single person in the room was laughing hysterically. Why? Because laughter is contagious!

Joy is contagious. Do you believe that? If so, ask yourself, who do you hang with? Are they the kind of people who have on their *dancing shoes?* If we want to be healthy, we have to build relationships with people who are willing to dance; and we have to be that kind of person, also. We can't just suck the joy out of people. We have to have it so we can give it away.

If we want to be able to give away joy, we have to know how to fill ourselves up with it first. All the years of building the church, plus the years of being married and raising three children has taught us some things about going through challenges. Being parents is not for the weak. Being in ministry is not just a bed of roses. Being married comes with its own set of unique challenges. Yes, it is a challenge to be a parent. We are challenged in our relationships, as friends, in our jobs; challenged with different health issues – In all those moments of life we can still, on purpose, have the spirit of joy.

At the very beginning of our dating life Casey and I recognized that we were both very serious-minded people. We like to be disciplined and have a strong work ethic. We also started out in our first years as Christians in a very, very strict discipleship group. Casey was involved with the Drug Rehabilitation Center where he had graduated, and he had become a staff member. They were not teasing about discipline and they worked all the time. We literally volunteered or worked every waking hour. We honestly slept no more than five hours a night and the rest was work, work, work; go, go, go – and there was definitely no room for fun.

As we began to grow as pastors, and as Christians, I realized we would not be able to continue along this pathway. Although we were very familiar with it – it was not what God wanted for us. It is easier to walk down the depression highway because people applaud the hard work. We all applaud diligence.

But we don't always applaud when a person fights to be joyful, because that can appear to be frivolous. Most of us would rather applaud the serious side of a person and all of their accomplishments, than applaud a person who seems to live on the frivolous side of life. We tend to put it down and say, *Oh, that's not very important.*

Let's ask the question: why does the Bible talk about joy and dancing, rejoicing and laughing? When we read our Bible we find there is dancing mentioned throughout the Bible. We not only find dancing, but rejoicing also. God shows us clearly that we are to rejoice at what He has done. We are to lift up our voices and sing. We are to dance before Him and make a joyful noise!

Learn to Smell the Roses

The funny thing is, Casey and I had to decide to let this area of what the Bible teaches us be part of our lives. Then we had to *discipline* ourselves to not always be so serious-minded. We had to remind ourselves to not get in this little hardnosed way of thinking and acting. We cannot forget to look up and smell the roses. First we *learned* how to smell the roses.

We learned how to start laughing by practicing. I honestly used to write on my teaching notes – smile! I literally wrote that in my notes for quite some time before each lesson I would teach. That is how serious it was to me. I truly wanted to renew my mind in this area of putting on my dancing shoes; of learning how to dance in life and not make everything so serious.

Through the course of my life I have practiced over and over and over putting on my dancing shoes. I want to be a person who allows joy to rise up on the inside to rule and reign in my life. I want to keep a place inside myself that is the little princess who is full of the wonder of her dress as she twirls. I want to be one who finds joy in the simple things of life.

Even though a hard situation comes at us, we need to allow the joy of the Lord to be our strength. We need to remember to allow His joy to rise up in us. Without the joy, we have no strength. So to have strength to overcome a situation we must practice walking in joy. When something seems very hard or we feel disappointed; when we feel frustrated about our parenting or inadequate at our job, that's when we *need to practice* the joy of the Lord. We can practice being lighter; changing our view of the situation by looking for something beautiful.

Lift up your head and look up, see what you can find that is beautiful. Change what you are focusing on in your life and begin to smile. You will begin to see things differently. You will honestly begin to smile. And when you smile, more joy will follow. Try this: On purpose try looking a person in the face, make eye contact, and smile! It is contagious! You will find most people will give that smile right back to you. And, suddenly you find, as you give and receive joy, you become stronger and it is so much easier!

I know many people think my personality is just open and friendly; I have the appearance of being happy to meet and visit with people. Usually, that is part of who I am. However, I have also needed to practice joyfulness over and over and over and over, until now it has become a habit in my life. It has become a part of me. As a result of developing this habit over the years, I now have the strength to help myself out when I am challenged to let heaviness take over.

Wearing our *dancing shoes* simply represents putting on the joy we might need at times. Our *dancing shoes* will cause us to sing or dance or laugh. Putting on our *dancing shoes* is watching something funny or getting out a joke book to tell jokes with your friends. Putting on our *dancing shoes* is spending time with a friend who has a light-hearted spirit.

Find Your Inside Smile

There are so many ways we can practice the *dance of life*. We must embrace the light-hearted joy of celebrating the good in our lives. The joy of the Lord isn't something we can put into a little tiny box and say, *this is what joy is.* I can't tell you, *this is how you get joy.* We all have to find what brings us joy. Joy is that inside smile. We each have to find what that means to us. Then we have to pursue those things that bring us joy.

Corrie Ten Boom has always been one of my heroes as a woman of faith. She was an older woman at the time she was taken prisoner during World War II. She was put into a horrible concentration camp where she lost her sister. Her father was also taken prisoner and died while in the concentration camp.

When she came out of the prison, she spoke of the filthy environment, and the horrible depravity of the people there. People were dying, starving, sickly, and being murdered all around her. Yet, she talked of finding a place in God; that place of peace and joy that can only come from our God while in the midst of such a horrendous situation.

Finding our joy isn't about everything around us being perfect. Everything won't always be all smooth, or without problems; in fact that would be quite rare. In the midst of darkness we can put on our dancing shoes and find *the smile of God* inside ourselves. Knowing that you have Him and He lives in you. That's true joy!

CHAPTER SIX

Your Very Own Glass Slipper

Your Very Own Glass Slipper

I can still remember the first time I bought a *really nice* pair of shoes. They weren't even high-end designer shoes, but they were the most expensive shoes I had ever purchased. Being a pastor's kid in a large family from Wenatchee, WA, I didn't grow up buying many new shoes, let alone really cool ones.

I can still picture them in my mind. They were navy blue high heels. I needed a pair of navy blue shoes, and when I saw this particular pair of shoes I thought they were the most beautiful shoes I had ever seen. I found them at Nordstrom and as soon as I saw them, I thought, *Oh my goodness. These are so beautiful.* I just knew I was going to buy them.

After I bought them, I definitely had buyer's remorse! I was so stressed! I had never spent so much money on one pair of shoes, and it felt so extravagant. Even though we had more than enough finances to cover the shoes, and I knew that God wanted us to live in abundance, I was not raised that way. My whole life we had never had much financially, so this shoe purchase really stretched me. It challenged how I thought about finances.

This is such a great visual picture to help us understand renewing our minds to the spirit of abundance. I was raised - as many of you were also – in a spirit of poverty. That place of *barely-get-by* that many of us have been programmed to expect and accept. It's what we grew up knowing. To help you understand the level of renewing I had to do, here is a picture of my childhood beliefs about finances. I didn't get my first new *store-bought* shirt until I was in sixth grade. I had plenty of used shirts, and pants and coats before then, but my first *store-bought* shirt was navy blue with white stripes – and I bought it brand new. I remember it perfectly, and I remember how I felt when I got it.

Receiving God's Abundance

Being raised in a pastor's home with six kids, my parents had to work hard and use faith to keep food on the table and clothes on everyone's backs. Even though all six of us shared one bicycle, we never felt we were lacking. I don't want it to sound like we were needy; or paint a picture of having a miserable childhood. We were raised in an amazing home, filled with love, and were never abused in any way. But, in the process of understanding the abundance of God, I have had to take time to renew my mind. I have had to work on my thinking due to the *lack mentality* of my childhood.

I have had to work on my thinking to not feel guilty about having enough finances. I have had to work at not feeling bad about receiving the abundance of God. I have had to work at not stopping the prosperity of God coming into my life, because I would think, *maybe God is going to be mad at me or people will judge me if I have abundance.*

I really do believe that the devil has used that kind of thinking to keep us in a place of lack. He likes us to be uncomfortable with finances. If we are uncomfortable with finances, we will not believe for more than enough. And if we will not believe for more than enough, we will not sow into the Kingdom of God. It's that simple.

Those Pearly Gates

Even though I loved my beautiful new blue shoes, I had some work to do on my thinking in order to be able to truly enjoy them. I believe our designer shoes can help us renew our minds to God's view of finances by visualizing the abundance of God. When God describes His home in Heaven, He describes streets of gold. Not just a little ring of gold. He's talking about entire streets made of solid gold! Have you seen anything like that here on earth?! God really goes for the magnificent!

He describes His gates as each one made from one pearl. Think about a pearl that is that huge! He has enough of those huge pearls to make several gates! Can you see how fabulous that gate is? It is simply beautiful beyond anything we have ever seen. If we saw a home on earth with the gate made out of a single pearl, we would call that extravagant. It is so beyond what we could imagine.

Most of us don't really have a true picture of what God thinks about finances, because our viewpoint is so small. What we think of as true designer shoes are really not that big of a deal in Heaven. We think we are so extravagant, when God says, Yes, a street of gold. No big deal. Yeah, *diamonds. What are they? Just some pretty little rocks. That pearl gate impresses you? It's just a beautiful little pearl to Me.* We let ourselves get all shook up over what we think of as extravagant, and God is not impressed. He created heaven and earth; and what He created is extravagant. It is elegant. It is beautiful. It is exceedingly abundantly above all that we could even think of or imagine.

When we learn to put on our *designer shoes,* I believe it helps us begin to see who our God really is, and what He wants for us, His daughters. Does it make you nervous to think of having a little extravagance in your life? When I talk about streets of gold, is your first thought, *I can't even meet my monthly bills. I need to fill up my tank with gas and it is going to cost me $50. Where am I going to get $50?*

If God can create so much beauty and abundance, do you really think He cannot or does not want to meet your needs? That is why I am even addressing the issue of *designer shoes.* We have to learn to think in terms of our Father God as our God of *more than enough.* But how do we change our thinking to be able to ask our abundant God to meet our earthly needs? What are the promises of God concerning finances and how do we access His Word to help with our needs?

What Does The Bible Teach About Money?

The question we have to ask ourselves is: *Do I even know what the Bible teaches about money?* We need to know what the Word says. We have all been taught certain principles about God and money growing up. I can confidently say, *Most of those were probably wrong.*

The Bible teaches us that He has a wonderful life waiting for us in Heaven, but, let's be practical – we need to know what is here for us on earth. He promises us a mansion when we get to Heaven, but let's be practical - we need to be able to pay for our house here on earth. We need to fill our gas tanks, and feed our families. For most of us, it is not too hard to believe God wants to meet *those* needs...just barely. But will He do more than that? That's where we often get stuck.

Remember, when I mentioned that in my study of God's Word, I always look for patterns? So, let's ask the question: Is that type of poverty thinking the pattern God shows us in the Bible? Are we supposed to live such an extravagant lifestyle that we are to have everything imaginable? Can we only have either one or the other? Are we not supposed to have extravagance? Are we supposed to live in poverty?

As we look for the patterns found in God's Word, we must ask God what He wants us to understand. The scriptures are all there, but we each need to ask some questions of ourselves and of God. Your thinking will determine how much of the Bible you will allow to be true in your life. So ask yourself some honest questions: *How do I really think I am supposed to live on this earth? Was I taught correctly? God what does Your Word really say?*

I got saved when I was 17 years old. One of the first things my youth pastor told me was, *The Bible teaches us to bring our tithe into the Church.* I said, *Oh! Okay.* Even though I had been raised in the church my whole life, I had never been taught about tithing. The minute he told me what the Bible taught, it was a done deal. That was when I began my adventure of understanding God's financial plan.

As I grew in the understanding of God's Word, I began to see how God wanted me to have more than enough. God wanted me to prosper even as my soul prospers (III John 2:1). God has given us the cattle on a thousand hills (Psalms 50:10). He wants me *to have* more than enough, so that I can *do* more than enough on this earth (Ephesians 3:20; Deuteronomy 8:18).

Historically Speaking...

The world of church history has given us the perspective that a true Christian will have nothing, live in poverty and because of that, God will love us more. We all know that the monks who deny themselves every earthly comfort are so much closer to God – right? But, is that God's point of view?

Many pastors and church leaders have preached and supported the lies of poverty thinking for centuries. It made me think: What if the Church had more than enough finances when TV came into existence? The Church could have owned the media airwaves and been able to preach The Gospel, instead of the secular media being the one to influence so much of our society. Instead of Christians being able to really get The Good News out there; we are limited by our poverty thinking. We can't get past the idea that money is evil and bad.

So, what did we do? We let the opportunity pass on by because Christian's thought having money was evil. Today, to preach the gospel on TV or other media costs millions. If we want to preach Jesus, we need to have vast resources of money available. Without resources, how will we get The Gospel preached in every nation?

The Root of All Evil

I honestly think we have had a reverse way of thinking about money. Instead of being afraid it will contaminate us, and make us suddenly turn evil, Christian's should have more money than anyone. I know poverty thinking has been propagated over and over; money is the root of all evil, we are told. We think if we have money, we will turn against God. It will tempt us and we will no longer serve God.

First of all, scripture says, *The love of money is the root of all evil* (I Timothy 6:1). It's not the money itself! Don't you think you can love God, serve Him and deal with the abundance He wants to give you? God wants to use us as avenues for good. He trusts us. He thinks we can handle having abundance, and that we will use it for good. *A good man leaves an inheritance to his children's children, but the wealth of the sinner is stored up for the righteous* (Proverbs 13:22).

He says a good man (or woman) leaves an inheritance for their grandchildren. He goes on to say that the wealth of the wicked is laid up for the righteous. That's us! He wants to put wealth into our hands. He trusts us to do right; He trusts us to help build His Kingdom. Why? So that we can do good works with it. He wants us to help and serve people with it. And...He wants us to have enough to give our children and their children a nice inheritance! That sounds like *designer shoes* to me!

Our *designer shoe* represents the exceeding abundance of God. There is nothing wrong with putting that designer shoe on, and enjoying it! We Christians have lived too long under the shadow of *if you have money then you must be doing something wrong.* It's amazing how we seem to judge anyone with wealth as a person who must be greedy or selfish.

God says in 2 Corinthians 9:8, *And God is able to make all grace abound toward you, that you, always having all sufficiency in all things, may have an abundance for every good work.* Ephesians 3:20 tells us, *Now to Him who is able to do exceedingly abundantly above all that we ask or think, according to the power that works in us.*

God Wants Us to Have More Than Enough

God wants to meet our need with more than enough abundance. So many of us have a belief in *just meet our bills,* and we live so that at the end of the month we have borrowed from Peter to pay Paul. We've just eaten the last of our macaroni and cheese – and now we are down to the Top Ramen.

We have this mentality of *less.* Then we are mad at those who have more. The whole thing that has happened in our country the last couple of years has been a fight against people who have abundance. Why? Bottom line, it is because we are full of greed, jealousy, and we want what someone else has. And if we can't have it, then they shouldn't have it either!

It's time for Christians to start believing what God's Word has to say. He says that we are supposed to have exceedingly abundantly above all that we could ask or think. Have you asked? Have you thought? Have you believed? Instead have we, as a group of people, decided that we are just going to be mad at anyone who has anything. Will we limit ourselves to being jealous and full of, *I want,* instead of full of God's abundance?

Malachi 3:10 teaches a very important principle when it comes to our *designer shoes*. It tells us, *Bring all the tithes into the storehouse, that there may be food in My house, and try Me now in this," says the Lord of hosts, "If I will not open for you the windows of heaven and pour out for you such blessing that there will not be room enough to receive it.*

We are all challenged when we first begin to believe what God's Word has to say about abundance. Most of us haven't seen it work in our lives. Our parents most likely did not teach us what the Word says and then train us to live it out. We've certainly heard people ridicule it. We've had people make fun of it. Few have positive thinking about living in abundance.

Bring the Tithe Into The Storehouse

Have you decided yet to try on your *designer shoes* for yourself? Even though you might be challenged, why not try it? The Bible says in Malachi to bring all the tithes. What is a tithe? It is ten percent of your income. Then it also says to bring all the tithes into *the storehouse*, which is your local church. We are to bring one tenth of our income into the church each week or month; whenever you are paid. We always take the first ten percent and set it aside for God's House, and then we pay our bills.

Why did God say to bring the tithe to the local church? We bring our tithe because the mission of the local church is helping people know Jesus. There is no other mission that we are to accomplish as Christians on this earth. There is no higher calling than to help people know Jesus.

Many people want to give money to help feed the poor or take care of the people on the street or help in a hurricane situation. These are challenging needs. We all want to help people who are in need, but this is a temporary fix. We want to help feed the outer person; we help give them shelter and clothing, as opposed to an eternal fix, which is Jesus! Tithing is about giving so that people will know Jesus.

If we feed them and they are filled in a physical sense, it is only temporary. They will be back again tomorrow, still needing to be fed. But if they don't know Jesus, they will die and go to hell. Let's be smart enough to give towards more than a full stomach. Let's give towards someone's eternity instead. I am not saying do not give to other needs, but I am saying that the tithe belongs to God's house, the church. After the tithe, we are free to give offerings as we choose.

Giving Will Change Your Future

The Bible teaches that not only does it matter where we give our finances, but also how we think about giving is important. 2 Corinthians says to give with a joyful heart, not just because we have to. *So let each one give as he purposes in his heart, not grudgingly or of necessity; for God loves a cheerful giver* (2 Corinthians 9:7). God wants us to be cheerful when we give. Not grudgingly; not because we have to give. Many of us may think, *It is easy for you to be cheerful as you give, you don't know how many bills I have to pay. You don't know how hard it is to get by and barely be able to get food on the table.* Even with all that going on, God wants us to give with a cheerful heart. When we do, He opens the windows of heaven and pours out a blessing on our lives.

You may feel it is impossible to begin to give, even just a little. You might think it wouldn't matter anyway. But, it does! You can change the outcome of how you are living your life from this day forward. You can change the long-term of what is going to happen in your future. Out of your own heart you are going to either plant a future filled with God's prosperity or out of your heart you will receive nothing. It is all based on your obedience to God's Word. Make the decision to be a person who tithes.

God Rebukes the Devourer

God also tells us in Malachi that when we tithe He rebukes the devourer for our sake. He stops the devourer from coming to steal from us. *And I will rebuke the devourer for your sakes, so that he will not destroy the fruit of your ground, nor shall the vine fail to bear fruit for you in the field, says the Lord of hosts; And all nations will call you blessed, for you will be a delightful land, says the Lord of hosts* (Malachi 3:11-12).

I can't tell you in my years of living as a Christian how many times God has rebuked the devourer for my sake. I have no idea how many problems have been diverted from my life. I don't know how many disasters have not happened that would have happened. I don't know how many of our things have lasted longer because of walking in God's blessing. I live under the blessing, so where I walk, the blessing of God follows. I always find the phenomenal sale. All because The Word says He will bless my life.

Look what God's Word says about the blessed life in the Book of Deuteronomy. *Blessed shall be the fruit of your body, the produce of your ground and the increase of your herds, the increase of your cattle and the offspring of your flocks. Blessed shall be your basket and your kneading bowl. Blessed shall you be when you come in, and blessed shall you be when you go out* (Deuteronomy 28:4-6).

In our world today, most of us don't have cattle or flocks. But, we do have a household full of needs. This amazing promise means the things I need for my household: my home, my food; my bills and of course, my *designer shoes* will be provided for. God helps me to find the best prices and He gives me what I need to make those purchases.

One of those really cool things I want to do in Heaven is ask God to show me all that He did to provide for me and my family. I think God will say, *Come on, Wendy. Come and see how I was able to provide for you in ways that were so beyond what you could ask or think.* Why? His Word is working exceedingly abundantly above all that I could ask or think, because I am a tither.

Don't Let Your Habits Drain Your Bank Account

Now in the area of finances – there are a few of us who are close to wrecking ourselves with our bad financial habits. We have developed certain habits in the area of our money and they are really not smart! We do the same thing over and over; we waste our money over and over without trying to gain any wisdom to make a change.

Many of us habitually use our money in the same way every month, without stopping to ask if there is a better way. We follow the example of our parents or the example of other people around us, without seeing if we really want the same results they are getting in their lives. We continue to get the same results they are, and we don't stop to ask a question. We don't demand of ourselves to evaluate what we are doing. We don't demand change.

If we want to make a change, we need to do something different! It is not easy to make a change. To have something different takes time; it takes discipline, learning and staying focused. Most people never change because most of us want everything to be easy – we want instant gratification. We want to plant the sapling apple tree one day, and see the tree full grown and producing fruit the next. Guess what? We don't get a mature, fruit bearing apple tree in a day.

Our beautiful Washington State is divided in half by the Cascade Mountain Range. The west side of the mountains is where we live now; it's the big cities, the Port of Seattle and the hub of busy city life in our area. It is absolutely beautiful! But, when I was younger I lived on the east side of the mountains, in the farming area of the state. I grew up seeing the farmers as they harvested of all the groves of apple trees and peach trees and cherry trees; but I also watched them as they first planted the trees.

Growth Takes Time

I have planted a few fruit trees in my yard over the years. I have had to wait years for fruit to grow from any of those trees. I would always look

111

at those trees, and tell them, *Come on, come on peach! Come on apple.* You know, first I had to plant this skinny little twig of a tree - it was just a spindly little nothing - then I had to water it, and put fertilizer on it. Then, I had to trim the branches each year. I've had to patiently watch it grow; and as it grew, I had to make sure I watched over it and took care of it.

In the area of finances, many times we just haven't taken the time to consider how to change what we are doing. In order to plant those trees, I had to learn something. I had to find out when the right time to plant was; where was the best location; what type of soil; do I water or do I not? The same is true with our finances. We need to ask ourselves, *What do I need to do to change?* What do we need to plant today so that in 5 years, 10 years and 20 years our children and grandchildren will be able to reap from the orchard in which we have planted?

That means we have to put a financial plan into action. Instead of spending every penny we ever make, we have to learn how to save and invest. I'm not just talking about tithing. We believe in tithing. But, there is much more to learn in order to be smart with our finances.

The Principle of NO!

Here is the biggest financial tip I can give you: learn how to use the simple principle called, NO! Go ahead and laugh. The brilliant *principle of no* means you have to say NO to yourself. There are times when we just can't buy everything we want. We don't get to go to the mall just because we say that is our hobby. If we go to the mall every time we get bored, all we do is keep buying, buying, and buying.

Oh, but it is such a sale. Yeah, but you put it on your credit card. Then you have to pay the interest on your credit card. By the time we get our credit card statement we don't actually pay off the dress that was at the amazing 50% off sale. When we actually do pay the credit card, that amazing dress we thought cost us $29.95, actually cost us $299.95 due to all the compounding interest! Many never think about the interest that accrues month after month. Many people live month to month, just making the minimum payment on more than one maxed out credit card! When we put that dress on our credit card, we don't include what it really costs to pay off that great deal; all because we wanted *instant gratification.*

Our American culture is so full of that *gimme, gimme, gimme* spirit. We just need everything immediately. We have become so accustomed to getting everything we want *right now* that we don't discipline ourselves to make a plan. We are undisciplined and we teach our children to act the same way. We don't teach them about making a plan, finding the best deal and then saving up the money to actually pay for what we want.

If this is you, and you really want to make a change, there are so many amazing financial teachers available to help. There are wonderful books and seminars to teach you the detailed information of how to better deal with your finances. I am not trying to give you that type of financial advice. I am simply sharing practical wisdom I have found in the Bible. Again, the biggest tip I could give you is how to say *no* to yourself.

Next, I think we also need to know how to say *yes* to ourselves. Remember, God wants to give us exceedingly abundantly more than we could ask or think, so make sure to have some fun, too. Having fun doesn't have to break the bank, but we do need to make sure there is something left for us. We need to have those small moments of pleasure that feed our soul. Take time for date nights; a pedicure; lunch with a friend once in awhile. Say *yes* to yourself – treat yourself as a daughter of the King of all kings. You deserve it!

A Woman Needs To Feel Secure

One of the major causes of divorce comes from having financial problems. Financial issues cause such friction in the home. There is so much stress and distress that comes with not having the bills paid and not knowing how you will make it through the month...again. Living in God's abundance will bring a sense of peace, a sense of assurance that we are being provided for. Women really need a feeling of financial security. A woman needs to feel secure, and God wants us to feel secure. He wants us to feel that He has provided more than enough for us. *Beloved, I pray that you may prosper in all things and be in health, just as your soul prospers* (3 John 1:2).

In order for our soul to prosper, we have to learn how to have abundance in our heart. It has to come from the inside of us; we can't get it from our husbands, or our children, or our job. The security we are seeking will only come through knowing God's Word and allowing His ways to be first in our lives. Is it hard? Sometimes it is very hard. But, it is a decision. It is our decision to make or not to make. Is it easy? No, it's not always easy. We just have to do it. Remember, we just have to get off the ledge and take that first step.

After all the years Casey and I have been tithing and giving I have found assurance in the knowledge that my actions are based on His Word. I feel there is a bigger mission in my life; instead of living for selfishness, or allowing myself to keep a *just-get-by* mentality, I know that God has blessed me to be a blessing. There is a security in knowing He is watching over me, to bless and prosper me; because I submit to His Word and His ways.

Take Back What the Devil Has Stolen

Buying that first new pair of shoes was something I did on purpose. I knew I needed help to stretch in the area of believing God had abundance for me. I knew I could not give away what I did not have for myself. I would not be able to believe for others what I was unwilling to believe for myself. The Bible teaches in Matthew 19:19, *You shall love your neighbor as yourself.* I knew I didn't love myself in the area of abundance. So I stretched myself to be able to believe for me, and to believe for you. I want us all to be able to say, *God has exceedingly abundantly provided for me.*

Stretching myself financially has caused me to believe to bring in more finances than I could have ever imagined. I have been able to grow and become stronger in taking back what the devil has stolen. I have a bigger than ever vision for Kingdom growth. I can see myself giving a higher percentage of my income than I ever would have been able to believe God for. I am passionate about how much I can bring in to build the Kingdom of God.

Casey and I have never given less than ten percent of our income. Our average giving for all of our married life is around 25 to 30% of our income every year. I don't say that to brag, I say that to stretch us. We stretch to help people. We give to further the Kingdom of God. But, we couldn't do that if we didn't first stretch ourselves to believe for a little bit more. What we allow God to bless us with will in turn help us to bless others.

Your Designer Shoes Aren't Just For You

The first time I wore my new blue shoes they were so amazing. I couldn't get over how nice they were. They were so beautiful. They were so comfy and fit perfectly. All I could think was, *Wow, God is so abundant.* As I look back on this story, I recognize that God used it to help me in the process of renewing my mind. It began the process of stretching me. From there I have been able to keep going and going.

Do we stretch and grow so we can have our nice *designer shoes?* No, we stretch and grow so we can build the Kingdom of God. This scripture in Deuteronomy says it best: *And you shall remember the Lord your God, for it is He who gives you power to get wealth, that He may establish His covenant which He swore to your fathers, as it is this day* (Deuteronomy 8:18).

Why do we put on our *designer shoes?* So we can rise up and show off the goodness of God. We can reflect the beauty and creativity of God. We can be the next Mary Kay of our generation. We can be the one who creates a business that puts hundreds of thousands of women into the workforce in a very positive way. We can be the one who brings great money into the Kingdom of God. Be the woman who is a part of something good. Not every person will create a

116

huge, successful company, but one will. We can all do what God has put in our hand to do; and use the money that God gives us to further the Kingdom of God. We need Christians, who understand the God-view of finances; who aren't afraid to be the ones to finance the Good News on this earth.

I love to learn the principles of God's ways by reading The Book of Proverbs. I read a chapter of Proverbs every day, and many of them deal with financial wisdom. I ask God to give me wisdom. To me that is putting on my *designer shoes!* I need the wisdom of God to know how to balance my life.

The balance in my life comes from this scripture: *Give, and it will be given to you: good measure, pressed down, shaken together, and running over will be put into your bosom. For with the same measure that you use, it will be measured back to you* (Luke 6:38). I want to be a woman who is generous. Not just in the financial realm. I want to give. I want to proudly wear my *designer shoes,* and be a woman who is giving and loving – with my spirit, my soul, my body, my emotions, and my finances.

CHAPTER SEVEN

Kick off Your Flip Flops

Kick Off Your Flip Flops

Flip, flop…flip, flop…flip, flop! I love the sound my *flip flop* shoes make as I walk towards the pool or down the beach. I don't know about you, but I don't wear my cheap little flip flops for very much other than a short walk to the pool. Those cheap, rubbery types of flip flops aren't very conducive to long shopping trips or walks of any distance. In fact, they aren't made to last and are pretty much a throw away type of shoe. And that is exactly what many Christians do – we throwaway God's Word as we *flip flop* through life.

Ask yourself this question: *How often do I just flip flop around in my beliefs?* Many of us, as Christians, put on our flip flop shoes every day – and it shows up in how we act. It shows up in what we choose to do…or not do. It says this in Galatians 4:9, *But now after you have known God, or rather are known by God, how is it that you turn again to the weak and beggarly elements, to which you desire again to be in bondage?*

As we come to know Jesus as Lord we declare, *Jesus, You are my Lord and Savior. I submit myself to You and will live my life according to Your Word;* and at the time we mean it! But, before too long, we begin sticking our foot back in the world's way of living. We have the idea we can straddle the fence when it comes to our lifestyle choices. We literally straddle the fence between living for Christ and living in the world. We want the best of both worlds, so instead of fully engaging in one or the other – we continuously *flip flop!*

Flip Flop Christianity Isn't New

We've all done it, so don't feel like you are an awful Christian if you have been guilty of wearing your *flip flop* shoes. Although it is not beneficial to us, it is also not uncommon. Christians have been flip flopping since the beginning of time. We saw it even as Jesus was being taken into custody; Peter denied Him three times. Jesus knew it would happen. Peter had just said he would never deny Jesus, and then within 24 hours...he denied Him three times! We see flip flop Christianity started even before Jesus was hung on the cross; and it has gone on throughout time. Living for God is not as easy as it seems. No matter how much we try, many of us just keep *flip flopping* back to our old worldly ways.

We *flip flop* for many reasons. Possibly we want to still be accepted by our worldly friends and family; or it could be we want to get ahead at our job, so we compromise our beliefs - not recognizing that by straddling the fence, we are not truly successful at either one. Instead, if we would fully engage in living out our Christianity, we would experience great joy and fulfillment. We would see that *the grass really is greener* if we would only leap over to God's side of the fence.

It says this in Galatians 3:1, *O foolish Galatians! Who has bewitched you that you should not obey the truth, before whose eyes Jesus Christ was clearly portrayed among you as crucified?* I love the way the writer says this. Who has bewitched you? Who has bewitched us as Christians? We know the truth, yet we have allowed ourselves to be tricked into doing wrong. We choose to live for our flesh, instead of living in the fullness of what God has for us.

Get Off The Sidelines

I do believe *we put on* our flip flop shoes. Those scriptures say we have been bewitched...which at first glance makes it look like we have no choice. But read further and you will see it is because *we have decided* to not obey the truth. I believe it is because we don't totally, one hundred percent engage in the things of God. We stand on the sidelines rather than jumping in to join the team. We aren't engaged in the serving, the giving, and the joy of being a Christian. Rather than fully live for Christ, we continue to live in the world. We get saved, and feel good for a few days, but if we continue to hang out with all our unsaved friends and relatives, we will continue to live as we always have. We will continue to straddle the fence; and that fence is just plain uncomfortable!

You may say, *I just want to go to the bar and have fun.* Well, do you not know how to have fun as a Christian? Have you not yet learned to have a joyful, open, happy relationship with the Christians around you? I have found that having fun is so much better as a Christian. We don't have to get drunk to engage in true laughter. Relationships are much deeper and more meaningful when they are based on serving people and loving God.

A lot of us, as Christians, want to *sit on the outside* of our relationship with God. Instead of really jumping in, we stay on the sidelines and watch. Jumping in feet first and engaging with the rest of the team is so much more rewarding than standing on the sidelines and watching. It's just so easy to be distracted and *bewitched,* when you are not playing on the team.

I think the devil gets happy when we stay on the sidelines. He laughs when we never fully engage with God and get the benefits of the peace that passes all understanding. He likes when we live never fully knowing the healing power of God in our spirit, our soul and our body. He likes us to stay disengaged to the point we don't have anyone to agree with us when we need prayer. And you know he is gleeful when we get mad, hurt or bitter towards the church.

Fire Escape Christianity

Another thing I honestly believe the flip flop mentality is based on is this: we only got saved to make sure we had fire insurance. You know, just in case it's true that there is a heaven and there is a hell. Just in case heaven is true and Jesus is real. We want to have the fire escape ready...*just in case.*

The world has convinced us that it is more fun to be living free and having *fun,* than being a Christian. And, sadly that is a common way of thinking. We are so convinced that committing our lives to Christ will take us down a long, dreary road to becoming sad, sorry, mean and boring. No fun at all! That is another lie the devil has perpetuated over the years. There is nothing more fulfilling, fun, joyous, and amazing than living for Christ!

I have to tell you the story of my brother, Scott. He was the first one in our family to be born again. My dad was a pastor so we spent our childhood going to church every week. We were raised to be moral people, but growing up we never heard the salvation message. My younger brother became born again when he was between 12 and 13 years of age. He was so excited and passionate for God after he was saved that we could all see a noticeable difference. In our denominational church salvation was a very private experience, and not something we ever really talked about.

When he was about 15 years old, I again saw a change in him. He totally turned his back on being a Christian. I was born again at 17 years of age, during my last year of high school, and I later went to Bible College. During these years I was separated from my younger brother because we lived in different cities so I didn't really see him much. I remember every time I did see him, he seemed so sad. There were several years when there was just a sense of darkness around him.

Scott had just finished high school and was going off to college when I next saw him. I was at work, selling shoes at J.C. Penney's, when my brother walked in the door. I looked up and I saw him way across on the other side of the store. As I watched him walk in the door, I saw his face - and there was a difference. His whole demeanor had changed. He looked like Scott again. I can't explain what it was about him, but he just looked happier.

After saying hello I had to say, "Scott, you look so different!" As I looked at him I knew what it was. I asked him, "Scott, have you gotten right with God?" He just looked at me and said, "How do you know that?" And I told him, "I could just tell by looking at your face." And he said, "I have."

I really wanted to know his story so I took a little break from work so he could tell me what had happened. He said, "I did know Jesus when I was younger. I was living for God, but I got so disheartened about certain things in the church, that I just stopped serving God. There was so much hypocrisy that I got discouraged." That is so sad and it is also very true.

Being in Church Doesn't Make You Perfect

Guess what? There are hypocrites in the church. Even though they come to church, some people are just not real. Sometimes there are people who are dishonest in the church. There are also people who are very judgmental – in the church. Yep, they are in the church. There are things that happen in the church that are not always the best. That's because we are all real people, who bring all of our good, bad and ugly with us into the church.

Many times we blame God for the imperfect people around us - simply because they are in the church. Just because you meet someone at church doesn't mean they are truly Christians. Meeting someone at church does not make them perfect. Because they are not perfect, that does not make Jesus imperfect. We get mad at God because of the imperfection of another human. And then we turn from God and walk away from the church.

What good does it do a person to leave the church? Doesn't that make them hypocritical too? There are all kinds of people who are hypocrites, whether they are in the church or outside of the church. We will meet people who seem to be hypocrites, but maybe they are just a baby Christian and haven't really learned how to walk with the Lord. Rather than get offended and judgmental, why not ask God for wisdom. I would rather be with the ones who are at least trying to be better by being in church.

Filling the Void Within

Scott was very young when he saw so much hypocrisy in the church. When he saw people he had trusted do things he considered wrong, it truly disheartened his soul, and he just walked away from the church. He turned his back on God and was drawn into a partying lifestyle. He thought that would fulfill him. I asked him, "What happened?" He answered, "You know Wendy, the problem was I couldn't do anything to fulfill that gap, that sadness inside. I tried but I just couldn't fill the void that came from being away from God. My friends, who didn't know Jesus, could drink a certain amount, but me – I couldn't drink the same amount they were drinking and get the same kind of feeling, because I had to drink more."

He continued, "I had to go further because I was running. I was running from having a relationship with the Creator of heaven and earth. I knew He had a mission for me and a life planned for me. It frustrated me because I knew it when it was happening. So I had to be a little bit wilder. I had to be a little bit crazier; my friends would seem to be satisfied with less, but I wasn't satisfied with less. I had to do more."

"Then it got to a place where I thought, *I can't do more.* It wasn't working to do more; I couldn't find any satisfaction within that lifestyle. So I had to ask myself, *What am I missing?* It came down to asking myself, *Who do you want to be? What do you want to live like?* I determined that I didn't want to live like this anymore. I was tired of the emptiness and trying to be satisfied with the world wasn't making me happy, because it was impossible."

Proverbs teaches us that there is a deep, dark pit that we can try to satisfy with the wages of sin; but it is impossible. The things we try to do to fulfill the empty place in our soul will not work; it is not possible. We cannot satisfy our soul with the world's ways; and yet the devil will try to tempt us. He will try to make the world seem so wonderful and so good and so satisfying.

All things have been delivered to Me by My Father, and no one knows the Son except the Father. Nor does anyone know the Father except the Son, and the one to whom the Son wills to reveal Him. Come to Me, all you who labor and are heavy laden, and I will give you rest. Take My yoke upon you and learn from Me, for I am gentle and lowly in heart, and you will find rest for your souls (Matthew 11:27-29).

Even At Our Worst, He Still Loves Us

This is the thing about God: He takes us even at our worst. He loves us even when we've been putting on our *flip flop shoes* – we've been good with God, bad with God, good with God, bad with God, good with God, bad with God. The thing is: His love doesn't fail. His love doesn't change. He says even though we have flip flopped and gone back and forth ten times, fifty times, or a hundred times – His love is still there.

Scott said, "All I did was turn around one day and say, *"God, You are right there. You've never left me. You've never forsaken me. Even though I have run from You – even though I have been unfaithful to You – You are right there."* He turned and gave his life back to God. I have to say the change was so evident, even in the demeanor of his face.

This is the thing about our *flip flop shoes:* we have to make an absolute determination that this is *our life;* and then pursue God. Once we make that decision The Holy Spirit inside of us will enable us to pursue it. Unfortunately, not all people will make the decision to commit to God and stay faithful to His Ways.

We are always going to find people who will continue putting on their *flip flop shoes* and be unfaithful. But my question is this: What are *you* going to do? You will always have people around you who are not faithful to the things of God. They will flip flop and never decide to really live for God. But will you?

Don't Turn Back

Psalms 78 talks about the people of God who have gone before us. For thousands of years people have built relationships with God. This psalm talks about the children of God being stubborn and rebellious. They did not set their heart right and were not faithful to God. They armed themselves, but they turned back on the day of battle.

And may not be like their fathers, a stubborn and rebellious generation, a generation that did not set its heart aright, and whose spirit was not faithful to God. The children of Ephraim, being armed and carrying bows, turned back in the day of battle. They did not keep the covenant of God; they refused to walk in His law, and forgot His works and His wonders that He had shown them. Marvelous things He did in the sight of their fathers, in the land of Egypt, in the field of Zion (Psalm 78:8-12).

They did not keep the covenant of God; they refused to walk in His law, and forgot His works. Will we forget His works? They forgot the wonders that He had shown them. God did marvelous things in the sight of their fathers, in the land of Egypt. They saw the things God had done to save His people, and yet instead of walking with God, they turned their backs on their covenant with Him. They had seen the works of God, yet they made a choice to turn back from His ways. They decided to find their satisfaction from the world.

We also have a choice and a decision to make every day. The result of our decision affects our family, it affects our finances, and it affects our emotions. Yes, there have been people we have looked at as our examples who may have flip flopped. We can use them as our excuse not to serve God. We may think, *If they can't do it, then I can't do it either.* The devil loves to applaud that way of thinking. He loves when we get discouraged and caught up in thinking about all those who have failed; he likes us to dwell on all the fakes, and all the phonies. He likes us thinking about the people who said they lived for God, but in reality they didn't.

Yes, there are many examples for us to use to justify our actions. We can build our case, and give ourselves the excuse, *if they can't do it, surely I can't either!* But, really it comes down to this: they are living their life and they will reap the result of their choices. Do you really want the result they will reap from living a *flip flop* life? Do you want the result that they are going to live? Galatians teaches us that what we sow is what we reap. *Do not be deceived, God is not mocked; for whatever a man sows, that he will also reap* (Galatians 6:7).

Develop Strong, Deep Roots

What are we planting towards our future? Are we planting towards a future full of success? Trees that stay planted develop deep roots. They will grow and produce beautiful, fully ripened fruit. As we flip flop it's impossible to develop strong, deep roots and bring forth healthy fruit in our lives. The *flip flop shoes* bring a small harvest into our future. When we stay steady and walk with God, our corn crop will produce big, beautiful stalks filled with growing ears of corn – and when we shuck the corn and take off the husk, we see beautiful yummy corn that is just so healthy looking.

The *flip flop shoes* produce something completely different. We may plant a seed towards our future, but then forget to water, or fertilize, or weed. That corn stalk might look good from the outside, but as we look closer, the inside is all dry and shriveled up. There is no healthy fruit, because there is no health in that corn. We haven't nurtured it, and we are reaping what we have sown.

We need to realize that our *flip flop* life is sowing seed into our future – into the future of our marriage, into the future of our children, into the future of our own growth. What we plant today is what we are going to reap tomorrow. It can seem like it's no big deal. If we only look directly in front of us, it doesn't seem like it's a big deal; but everything that we do today plants a seed for tomorrow.

Through Thick and Thin

My desire is for each and every one of us to no longer be bewitched by the lies that earth life is more valuable than our relationship with Almighty God. What the devil sets before us is nothing compared to what we can receive from knowing God. I would love each of us to say, *I am no longer going to see the promises of God and ignore them or turn my back on them.* Instead of being the person that Galatians was talking about, say *I will not be bewitched. I will not turn away from obeying the truth, but will be a person who pursues the things of God.*

In Casey's and my Bible school days, the founder of our Bible school, Pastor Johnson, had a beautiful poem that I would love to share with you. (I was just 18 years old and Pastor Johnson was a great-grandfather at this point in his life. He was a great man who had a special twinkle in his eye; a man who walked the walk of faith and although he had lived through difficult trials and tribulations, he would always have that twinkle.) It is the best poem that he taught us in our four years of Bible school. He would look at all us young students, who were just beginning our walk with Christ, and he would say, *This is my poem of life and this is how you can have success:*

Plod on, plod on, plod on and plod on.

And that is what I would say to each one of us. Don't be bewitched with the ways of the world. Don't be tricked into thinking that a life of partying and doing other things will fulfill you; don't think trying to get ahead on your own strength and having all that this world has to offer, will bring you peace.

Instead plant the kind of field you want to harvest from; stop putting on your *flip flop shoes*. Decide to pursue the things of God one hundred percent. Decide to plant a field of kindness, generosity, more than enough, faithfulness, and security in God. Decide to know what the Word of God has to say; through thick and thin, stay true to Him. Live by the principles of life found in God's Word. Instead of *flip flopping* - plod on, plod on, and plod on.

CHAPTER EIGHT

Watch Your Step

Watch Your Step

It seems to be the dream of every little girl to wear *high heel shoes*. I'm sure we could all tell our story of our first pair of high heels. If you were a young girl receiving your first pair of your own little plastic high heels it was probably your *dream-come-true*. (Anyone remember the pain from wearing them too long the first day you got them?) We were so glamorous and grown up in those little plastic shoes!

Maybe you remember your first time wearing high heels was playing dress up with your mom's things. As we don our mom's high heels for the first time we are oh-so-careful as we begin to walk. We realize, as beautiful as they are, these shoes are dangerous! And wobbly! We realize we could fall! But the danger is worth the glamour and beauty we feel when we wear our high heels. Have you ever noticed how wearing high heels makes us feel? They can make us feel pretty, stately, and just plain put together. They can pull our outfit together and boost our confidence at the same time. While everyone doesn't like wearing high heels, I do. My husband, Casey, is really tall so I've gotten used to wearing them.

Walking In Heels Takes Practice!

Wearing high heels takes practice. Beautiful as they are, it takes time to master walking in them. We need to figure out how to stay balanced and walk at the same time! We need to figure out how we are going to strut up those steps or walk down that hill. To me, high heels represent how we must remain careful and cautious about where we are walking in life. We must carefully ponder how to keep our walk with God on track.

There are always little cracks in the sidewalk that can trip us up. We can be walking along, and hit a tiny little bump in the road and – boom - that heel gets caught and down we go! You may think, *I have this huge, flat sidewalk to walk on, and I find that one little crack?* I think this happens to us in life more than we realize.

Like a beautiful pair of heels, there are things in the world that can appeal to us, but if we do not pay attention, we may step where we shouldn't. Those things have the ability to take us down. We need to be very, very cautious about what we choose to do, where we go and who we hang with along the way. Those small choices can trip us up and take us out of running our race for Christ. Many times, we don't even see it coming.

Watch Where You Are Going

I have tried on high heels that looked wonderful, but once I got them on, I found myself tripping all over the place. They didn't fit right. They weren't comfortable and I could not walk correctly in them. In the same way, we must be cautious about what we view as attractive, and listen to God with our conscience to make right choices. Listen to that still small voice on the inside that is telling you, *Don't go to that place. Those aren't the type of people you should spend time with.* That voice is the Holy Spirit trying to guide your steps.

God's Word tells us that we are to walk carefully as wise, godly women. It says in 1 Thessalonians 5:6, *Therefore let us not sleep, as others do, but let us watch and be sober.* 1 Peter 4:7 reads, *But, the end of all things is at hand; therefore be serious and watchful in your prayers.* Notice the emphasis on being watchful and sober. Our Father God knows there are all kinds of pitfalls out there. There are rocks in the road, grooves in the pavement and uneven places that can trip us up. We have to slow down and pay attention to where we are walking. That is why we must be sober. Watch what you are doing, and be aware of what is going on in life.

Many of us, especially in America, are extremely spoiled. We want everything our way, we want it fast and we want it perfect. We want to have our cake and eat it too – with soft-serve ice cream! Many have never traveled beyond our country's borders and seen how other people live. We think everything is supposed to work in our favor, and everyone should take care of us. We don't feel we should have to make hard decisions, choose our friends wisely, or pray and be involved with church. We want everything to come easy. Sadly, when something is too easy it is also usually cheap. It is counterfeit. Kind of like those cheap little plastic heels we once adored.

Don't Settle for an Imitation

By not making the hard choices and choosing what builds us up, we settle for an imitation. We just run through life not recognizing that we cannot run in our *high heels* without running into a problem. It says in,

1 Corinthians 6:12, *All things are lawful for me, but all things are not helpful. All things are lawful for me, but I will not be brought under the power of any.* There are many things we can do, but does it really help us in the long run? For example, it is okay for us to watch whatever we want on TV. It is okay for us to read whatever we want. It is permissible for us to skip doing the God things of life – praying, reading the Word, being in church – it is permissible. God gave us a free will. We are still saved, but, do our choices really help us?

As powerful women, we must be smart. We have on these high heels, and they are beautiful, but we have to watch our step. We have a choice to make. We decide, *I can do whatever I want because the Bible says, everything is permissible.* That includes drinking, smoking, and using drugs. That is all permissible. We can read the latest X-rated novels and it is permissible. We can watch scary, thriller movies, and it is permissible. We can even watch movies with rape and murder in them. But, if we fill our minds with that stuff, our *high heels* will eventually get stuck in the crevasses. We will trip ourselves up because we are not being sober as Thessalonians teaches us. God's Word says we must watch and pray. Watch where you are walking, and how you are stepping.

You Can...But Should You?

There are many things which are permissible; but is it profitable for you? Does it really benefit you in the long term of your life? Does it help you be a better wife, mom, friend and Christian? We need to ask ourselves, *What am I doing in my life today that I want to reap in years to come?* When we are watching certain things and hanging around certain people, we must challenge ourselves, *What am I sowing? What seeds am I planting that will bring forth future fruit?*

You say, *Yeah, but I just want to go to the club. I want to keep smoking. I want to hang out. I want to eat whatever I want to eat.* Yes, it is permissible, but is it profitable? None of those things will send you to hell. You can absolutely do them. But, what will that get you in the end? I have learned from leading our church and being a Christian for many, many years that when a person does something because they *have to,* or because they think God will love them more if they do it, they don't really change. There may be a temporary fix, but they very quickly go back to doing what they want to do.

We are all going to do what we want to do, but please listen: we each must decide at the beginning of our relationship with Jesus which pathway we want to walk. I consciously chose to be a person who was watchful and sober. Why? I wanted to produce great fruit in my life. I wanted to be an example to the world that Jesus loves me, and I walk in His grace, mercy and truth. My love for people was more important than the *things* I might have wanted to do.

I *could* do what the world does, but I choose not to. Why? I like the results of my choices better! Instead of watching scary TV shows and sowing fear into my heart; I did not do it, and it helped my heart stay at peace. Instead of worrying about changes in the economy, I choose to believe my God is more than enough. I just had to make certain decisions. I usually do not watch the news. Honestly, I find it to be mostly bad news. I want to live at peace, so I limit what I watch and how much I watch.

What Are You Sowing Into Your Heart?

Many years ago, Casey and I looked at how much sickness and disease was around us. As a result, we stopped watching medical shows. Let me just say right away that it is permissible to watch those kinds of shows. It doesn't make us evil, and it doesn't make us bad; but what are we sowing into our hearts? We wanted to be healthy and live a long, healthy life, and while it was permissible for us to watch those medical shows, it was not profitable. It gave more opportunity for the enemy to bring back to our minds those negative, unhealthy situations. It just planted visual seeds of sickness and disease that we did not want in our minds.

That decision eliminated other distractions like the advertisements that came along with the TV shows. Many commercials are just medicine, medicine, and more medicine! Not only the medicine, but my goodness – all those side effects! We decided that when those ads came on, we would mute the TV. Now, we purposefully mute it or if we DVR it, we just fast forward so we don't see it and sow those thoughts into our minds. Again it is permissible, but is it profitable?

Something happened in my Christian walk early on to really cement this principle within my heart and mind, and I'd like to share it with you. I like cigarette smoke. I don't smoke now, but just before I got saved I was a bit of a smoker. I had not become an addictive smoker because I was so young, but I liked smoking. One day I was with one of my unsaved friends, and I was smoking. She just looked at me and said, *Here you are smoking a cigarette. What kind of Christian example is that?* I could have said to her,

Hey, this is no big deal. I'm still going to heaven. After all, smoking was permissible for me, but the Word says we are to watch our behavior as daughters of Almighty God.

When she said that to me, I looked at the cigarette in my hand, and I looked at her, and I just dropped the cigarette on the ground. That was the last time I smoked. Isn't it amazing how well the unsaved know what is right and wrong for Christians to do? It only took me a minute to decide my friend was worth more than my desire to smoke. I knew she was judging the authenticity of my walk with Christ by my actions. Sure, it was permissible, but that was not profitable for me.

Who Do You Want to Be?

I had great plans for who I wanted to be. I had a vision of how I was going to represent my Savior. We each must have a vision and a mental picture of the kind of women we want to be. Not based on I *have to,* but based on I *want to.* Decide the kind of woman you want to be and choose how you will wear those high heels. How will you maneuver the cracks in the pavement? How will you prevent yourself from getting caught in the places where the devil wants to trip you up?

We make lifestyle choices on the principle of walking carefully. Walk soberly, not because you've been forced to, but because you've made a choice. Be the kind of God-woman that doesn't rely upon what the world has to give. Walk confidently, strong and tall, showing forth the light of Jesus in your amazing *high heel shoes.*

Just as we choose different heels for different occasions, each of us chooses how we will handle life's situations based on our level of intimacy with God. When we are close with God, we are more confident in our decisions. Many of us are saved. We love Jesus, and over the days, weeks and months of our journey with Christ, we find that we are stronger and closer to God. We're diligently reading the Word, praying without ceasing and our relationships with other Christians and with church are thriving. But, sometimes our light gets a little dim. And when our light is dim we make choices differently from what we would have done previously.

His Love Is Never-Ending

The good news is that even when we become weak in our relationship with Him, God's love for us never grows dim. It is just as bright as the day we were born. His love for us remains steadfast and consistent, but our response to Him, and our ability to hear His voice may not always be sharp. We are not always sensitive to hearing how we should handle situations. Sometimes instead of putting on our walking shoes, we've put on our running shoes. Sometimes we put on our dancing shoes, instead of our boxing shoes. Sometimes we put on our high heels, but we should have worn our little flat shoes. Our choices aren't perfect, but God still loves us.

That's where Romans 12:2 comes into play, *And do not be conformed to this world, but be transformed by the renewing of your mind, that you may prove what is that good and acceptable and perfect will of God.* We honestly want to do the good, the acceptable and the perfect will of God. Our heart is right, but our spirit has grown a little dim. We aren't hearing

God's voice the way we did at one time. We have let our high heels get a little wobbly again, because we have lost our strength; we've lost the ability to walk straight and strong.

There will be times when our choice is a *good* choice, but it isn't necessarily the best choice. As we press more into His presence, we will more clearly hear His voice and better understand His perfect will. God's Word and His love never change. Regardless of whether we make the best choice or not, God loves us! If we make an acceptable choice, God still loves us! When we make the perfect choice, God loves us the same! His love does not change based on our choices. His love remains the same whether we walk strong in our *high heel shoes* or when we wobble around a bit. The key is to keep walking in His love!

CHAPTER NINE

Small Shoes, Big Faith

Small Shoes, Big Faith

It's been many years since I have purchased *little kid shoes!* My kids are way past that stage, but since I am now a first-time grandma, I have begun to look at these tiny, sweet little shoes again. When I think of *little kid shoes* I picture the innocence and sweetness of a new life. Can't you just imagine the smell of a tiny baby, all powdery and soft? Can you hear the happy, giggling sound of a small child? To me these images bring with them a sense of innocence and total trust. These tiny shoes show me the vulnerability we should wear as children of God. We are to be dependent upon Him, but more importantly, we are to be full of trust.

We all know those tiny little baby shoes are just for the mom, to make her feel good...because they are all show and no substance. Our kids don't start out walking in those kinds of shoes. As they begin to grow and learn to walk they need something sturdier for their feet, and they need to let their mom and dad hold their hand. They need their daddy to help steady them as they begin to take their first steps. Just as that small child needs their daddy, we also need our Daddy God to help us. He wants us to feel secure in knowing He is there to keep us safe. He wants to have a Father – Child relationship with us.

Jesus gave us the perfect viewpoint of what the Father wants from His children. *At that time the disciples came to Jesus, saying, "Who then is greatest in the kingdom of heaven?" Then Jesus called a little child to Him, set him in the midst of them, and said, "Assuredly, I say to you, unless you are converted and become as little children, you will by no means enter the kingdom of heaven. Therefore whoever humbles himself as this little child is the greatest in the kingdom of heaven. Whoever receives one little child like this in My name receives Me* (Matthew 18:1-5).

He Wants Our Trust

In order to be like a child on this earth, we need to regularly put on our *little kid shoes.* What does that mean? We need to humble ourselves and see ourselves as children in the eyes of God. The more child-like we can be in our vulnerability toward God, the more we will have the ability to trust Him. A child has trust. A child has the innocence of believing. Just look at the innocence of the little children around you; that is exactly what God wants from us as His kids.

As we mature we have the tendency to pull back our trust. God tells us, *Go ahead. You can do it.* And we say, *I don't think so.* Our first response is, *No! I can't. It's not possible.* Why? We have lost the ability to trust. We no longer see ourselves in our *little kid shoes;* we've forgotten to walk through life holding our Father's hand.

Through time many of us lose our ability to be vulnerable with God. We've forgotten He is our Abba Father. In Romans 8:15 it says, *For you did not receive the spirit of bondage again to fear, but you received the Spirit of adoption by whom we cry out, Abba, Father.* Instead of innocence and trust, we have learned to live guarded and fearful. We did not receive fear when we received Christ; we received the Spirit of adoption, by whom we cry out, Abba, Father. He is our *Daddy God.*

Daddy God Wants to Hold You in His Arms

When we think of a *daddy,* what do we picture in our minds? I see a little girl climbing up in her daddy's lap, full of the confidence that she will be wanted, comforted and loved. I see snuggles and tickles and hugs. I see trust and a sense of knowing everything will be fine now that *daddy* has us. But that is not what every woman sees when she thinks of what a daddy is – she sees a different picture in her mind.

Why is it so difficult for some of us to embrace a loving relationship with Father God? It can be because of the relationship we had with our earthly father. It has been said that most of us perceive Father God the same way we perceive our earthly father. When we hear Daddy God or Father God, our minds just shut off. We don't know how to have a comfortable relationship with Him. Our viewpoint is skewed by the problems and hurts of what we learned from our earthly dad. The ability to trust our earthly father has been twisted by neglect, abuse or other problems, and we cannot see Father God any differently. Our earthly father was never there; he didn't respond when we needed him; therefore, we don't believe Father God will respond either.

I would guess that at least 50% of women did not have a healthy father/ daughter relationship growing up. Their dad was either abusive, absent mentally or was not physically present in their life. Maybe their dad wasn't around for most of their life. We have all heard the stories or seen the different TV shows where a woman tries to find the father she never knew. It always sounds very sweet and touching to witness a reunion like that. They go into the situation with such high hopes; and probably once in a blue moon there is true success. But, in most cases, it is a bomb.

It would be great for every little girl to have the perfect fairy-tale ending; to find their perfect father and become Daddy's little princess. What happens most often though, is their father either didn't want them or his life is such a disaster he has no ability to really love and nurture them. They have nothing to give us, and yet we have this hunger to have a relationship with our father.

Many women have married the wrong man, because without really knowing it, they are trying to replace the father they never had. Instead of getting the father figure they pictured in their mind, they end up with a man who abuses and neglects them. I wonder how many of us can relate to neglect and abuse more easily than we can to someone who loves and nurtures us. We become trapped in a place of hurt, and are without the ability to reach beyond the pain to let Daddy God bring healing into our hearts. We cannot sit on Daddy God's lap and receive the acceptance and love He has for us. It is just too vulnerable.

I understand that feeling of vulnerability. Feeling vulnerable is just so...unsafe. It is unsafe because when we are vulnerable, we can be hurt. If someone knows something about us, they can use it against us. If we open our hearts to someone, then they have the power to hurt us. How many times were we vulnerable with our father and he laughed at us? How often did we expose our feelings to our husband, and he used those feelings against us? We let ourselves become vulnerable and we were hurt. We trusted someone and they didn't come through. They betrayed us for somebody else. There was violence. There was abuse. Our vulnerability was met with betrayal.

Remind Yourself of Who You Are

As daughters of the King of Kings, we can remind ourselves who we are. It is our right, as a daughter of Almighty God, to have victory in our life. We have relationship with our Abba Father, who will never leave us or forsake us. He cannot let us down. We need to truly know that God loves us. He tells us, *I will not leave you orphans; I will come to you* (John 14:18).

He also says, *No longer do I call you servants, for a servant does not know what his master is doing; but I have called you friends, for all things that I heard from My Father I have made known to you. You did not choose Me, but I chose you and appointed you that you should go and bear fruit, and that your fruit should remain, that whatever you ask the Father in My name He may give you. These things I command you, that you love one another* (John 15:15-17).

He has chosen us! He wants to be our Daddy God. He has chosen us as His daughters, to live forever with Him. He will never give up on us, never hurt or abuse us; He doesn't have the ability to cause us pain. He is love; and He has chosen to give that love to us! That is wonderful, but there is also something about us choosing God. Have you considered that you also need to choose to believe what He sees in you? We each have to choose to see that we are His daughter, to accept that we have been chosen by Him, that we are wanted by Him.

You are Wonderfully Made

I love this scripture in Psalms which says we have been fearfully and wonderfully made: *For You formed my inward parts; You covered me in my mother's womb. I will praise You, for I am fearfully and wonderfully made; marvelous are Your works, and that my soul knows very well. My frame was not hidden from You, when I was made in secret, and skillfully wrought in the lowest parts of the earth* (Psalm 139:13-15).

The writer says, *Marvelous are Your works...* And we want to say, *Are you kidding me?* When we read that, many of us want to ask, *What's marvelous about me?* We don't always say the words out loud, but we say it in our hearts. We say, *Right, God. You don't really know me. If You really knew what I was like, You would not be saying that about me.* As if God doesn't know everything. He knows every moment of your life and He still chose you.

God not only says, *I have fearfully and wonderfully made you,* but He adds on top of it, *And marvelous are My works.* Marvelous, amazing, beautiful are My works. Why not try looking in a mirror with God's thoughts. Try looking with a plan to renew your mind; exchanging the way you think for what God says about you. We have to decide, *I'm going to change the way I think. I'm going to start believing what God says about me.* We need to decide to stop identifying with our earthly father's view and connect with what our Heavenly Father says about us. We need to put on our *little kid shoes,* and choose something new for our future.

In choosing something new for our future, I want to say that we will not change our past overnight. Our Christian walk is not about reading a book like this, seeing the things we need to change and then, magically we're done! *All fixed - mind renewed. I am complete.* That is not what being a Christian is about. Christianity is a journey in which we walk day-by-day, with the Bible as our guidebook.

To help us on our journey we need to get revelation from God's Word. As we read our Bible – His Rhema Word becomes alive and powerful to help us on our journey. That is why I read my Bible every day. Not to complete a yearly Bible reading plan, but to get revelation knowledge from God's Word for me. God speaks to my heart as He quickens His Word to bring peace, healing, and wisdom for all the areas of my life. In my journey of life, if I do not read my Bible, I'm not getting food to help me along my way.

Another part of our journey to becoming a stronger woman is being around church and building godly relationships. Our church friends are a part of our journey of growth. We must have strong Christian friendships to help us get to a place of really knowing God. Christianity is not supposed to be a lonely journey, nor is it done in a moment of time. No, it is a daily journey of getting one thing figured out, and then a new revelation about another situation becomes clear. We continually put on our *little kid shoes,* as we daily renew our minds to who we are in Father God's eyes.

It Takes Time

Some of us come from such extreme issues in our backgrounds. I would never try to tell you that you should be able to deal with those issues in a short amount of time. Don't ever let anyone put you down for where you are at on your journey with Christ. That is so contrary to the very nature and love of our God. He gently leads us, day-by-day, and situation-by-situation. The very nature of God is healing. When someone made an evil choice and did evil against you, God didn't turn His back on you. He is right there to bring about healing in every area of your past. He wants to bring you a new way of thinking about your future. He wants to help you put on your *little kid shoes* to help you walk through the hurt and pain, into His healing.

I grew up with a great dad. I always knew I was a favorite of his, and I had a good relationship with him. We didn't have great conversations because he wasn't that kind of a dad, but he was very warm and affectionate towards me. On my journey of seeing Father God in a healthy way, I have had less ground to cover. Some of you have more ground to cover; and you will have to decide *–this journey is about God and me daily coming to a place of wholeness and health. This is my journey and this is my walk with God.* Whether you are at the beginning or the middle of your journey, make the choice to have health in your life.

SMALL SHOES, BIG FAITH

My desire and dream is for you to get a fresh view of what God has for you. We can change our view. In doing so, we will begin to walk in a place of freedom. He wants us to be able to renew the spirit of our mind, in order to be able to act differently on this earth. Those who have been abused carry a tattoo of that abuse on their soul. Those who live with a feeling of being abandoned recognize they have the heart of an orphan that affects their personality. They often feel separated, alone, betrayed, or abandoned. It is hard for them to truly trust others.

God says, *I have not left you orphans.* He wants to fill that void in our hearts. He wants to help us begin to be able to see ourselves as a little child again. As we put on our *little kid shoes,* we will see through the eyes of trust and start to believe we are loved. As we begin to believe in the love God has for us, we will begin to love others. We can love, because we are loved. If we can only see that we have been abused, that is exactly what we will give away to other people.

Renewing Our Innocence

In order to move beyond the hurt of our past we cannot just ignore what we've lived through. To me the terminology, *forgive and forget* is kind of ridiculous. We don't forget the situations that we've walked through. No one forgets if they were abused or had a trauma in their life. Although we don't forget, we can learn from all of those situations. We can use those hard situations to become stronger as a person. We gain wisdom from all that we have experienced.

Life will give us all kinds of wisdom, but we have to be careful of becoming cynical and hard. That's why we put on our *little kid shoes* every day. The God-part of being a child says *I will forgive.* It is impossible to forgive if we try to do it on our own. But, as we see through the eyes of a child, forgiveness comes easier. We ask Father God to help us, because there is no way we can forgive on our own.

Too many Christians, simply try to just *gut it out.* We try to do it alone. We do not have the ability to forgive on our own, but we do have the ability to call out to God. We are to live a life of forgiveness; we have been told to forgive seventy times seven. *Then Peter came to Him and said, "Lord, how often shall my brother sin against me, and I forgive him? Up to seven times?" Jesus said to him, "I do not say to you, up to seven times, but up to seventy times seven"* (Matthew 18:21-22).

We have the ability to forgive because He said we can. As we put on our little kid shoes our ability to forgive increases. We have a hard time forgiving in our cynical, unforgiving, adult way of thinking. But, we can do it when we allow the Spirit of God to bring us to a place of innocence in Him; a place of vulnerability, of knowing we also need His forgiveness in our lives. We would all walk down those same pathways and do the things in need of forgiveness without Jesus by our side. Be careful of throwing stones. Allow God to let you see through the eyes of a child.

When I think of *little kid shoes,* I see the eyes of a child; eyes full of faith, eyes filled with love, eyes that are trusting, eyes which believe. I see eyes which communicate, *I belong – I am not an abandoned child. I'm not a neglected child. I'm not an unwanted child. I am a loved woman.*

Seeing Through the Eyes of a Child

Our *little kids' shoes* communicate that starry-eyed, trusting, child-like *belief.* I'm talking about the kind of belief that doesn't always have to figure everything out; because a child doesn't figure everything out first. They just believe. A child doesn't make sure they know how everything is going to happen. We need to have that same child-like faith as we follow God. By faith, we say *yes* to God's ways. As we decide to walk in our *little kids shoes,* we need to ask – how would a child see the situation? By seeing with the eyes of child-like faith, we can begin to call those things that are not as though they are.

The Word says... *(as it is written, "I have made you a father of many nations") in the presence of Him whom he believed—God, who gives life to the dead and calls those things which do not exist as though they did...* (Romans 4:17).

As we trust more in our child-like faith, we begin to act more on God's Word. This is the faith way of living. It is the way God has called us to live. Sure, we are adults and we have walked through many adult situations. We might even be old enough to have children who are married and they have children of their own. Our little kid shoes are not only for the newly saved or those under a certain age. We are talking about remembering in the midst of every situation to see through the eyes of a child, and trust our Daddy God still has the answer.

Lessons from a Child

1. Children Love to Explore and Learn

I love to be around kids. They have such innocence, such energy, and curiosity. They love to learn and explore - and they love to try new things. Many of us are never around an environment where there are children. I would encourage you to make a way to get around children and learn from them. Children are very willing to just do things. It is very intriguing to watch a child; it's amazing to see their thought process. Sometimes I just have to shake my head and wonder, *why are they doing that?* Just seeing the inquisitiveness of a child is a good reminder for us to live our life full of the joy of learning and growing.

2. The Generosity of a Child

The generosity of a child is beautiful to see. Watch a little child who has been given a handful of pennies. Those pennies could be their most prized possession, yet what will they do? Most children will give their pennies away. Oh, yeah, they will just give them all away. They want us to have what they have, because they have spirit of generosity. The sad truth is, as children get older, they begin to want to keep all their pennies. And as we mature into adulthood, we live a life of keeping all our pennies. We keep them because we value our pennies more than we value people, or value the things of God.

As we view the heart of a child we see such innate generosity. They are generous in their love. They are generous in their kindness. There is a generosity in their efforts to help. If somebody needs help, they are right there. It is amazing; just watch a small child whose sibling needs help. They will call, *Mom, Mom – come, come*. They *need* to get Mom to come and help. They want to be a part of it. They don't run from a need. If someone is in pain a child never runs and hides. They run to them and they will help or they will get somebody to help. God has placed that quality in us as children – it is the heart of God.

Don't you love the sweetness of how a child will just come up and hug your leg? They don't think about, *should I or should I not*. It never crosses their minds that they might be rejected. They just have that sweet little smile and there is such innocence in their actions; they express very simply what is in their hearts.

We can also learn how to have that same sweet innocence in our relationships of life. As we grow older we begin to put our guard up and it's harder to be open with others. We don't want to be rejected, so we pull back. That is another way the devil keeps us from giving into the lives of others. We allow the fear of rejection to hold us hostage. Instead, remember to put on your *little kid shoes* and freely give yourself to love and help people.

3. The Freedom of a Child

Children are also profound in how they worship God. Watch a child lift their hands and dance around freely. They don't wonder, *am I keeping the beat; am I looking good; is my hair just right* – they don't think in those terms. Children just freely worship. They are so free in their emotions – if they are going to cry – there is honesty in their crying. They cry and then they are done.

There is freedom in the spirit, soul, and body of a child. Some children are just fearless. They will give everything they've got to what they are doing – whether on a trampoline or a bike – and they will just *go* because there is a sense of fearlessness about them. Eventually we will watch a child change, and they will begin to become more cautious. That fearlessness begins to leave them.

We begin to lose some of our fearlessness as we mature. Many times it is out of wisdom that we make new choices. But, as we acquire wisdom, we must also remember to not leave behind the attitude of our *little kid shoes*. We have to blend the understanding of maturity with looking through the eyes of a child. Are we generous or is there sense of stinginess about us? In your soul, do you have a spirit of generosity when a person is in pain or when they are experiencing joy? Do you celebrate with them and do what you can to serve and help, or do you withdraw and pull yourself back?

There is wisdom to be found in looking at the innocence of a child. There is balance in looking at life through the eyes of a child. When we are looking at all the different areas of giving in our spirit, our soul, our body, our finances, our emotions, our relationships, our serving, and our giving – make sure to look through the eyes of a child. Keep your heart fresh and alive to the ways of God. Remember to put on your *little kid shoes,* and keep a spirit of innocence in your life.

CHAPTER TEN

With These Shoes I Thee Wed

With These Shoes I Thee Wed

I have been married for over 35 years – and guess what? I still like my husband. Just as important, my husband still likes me, too! The reason we have had a long, successful marriage is we have put on our *marriage shoes* correctly. We have, on purpose, lived a life that at 35 years of marriage is happy, fulfilling and going strong. So we can confidently say that at 50 years of marriage, and at 70 years of marriage, and then maybe even 80 or 90 years of marriage, we will have a solid marriage. We will still love being married!

Let me start off with this comment: *I am great at wearing my marriage shoes. I am a person you should be listening to.* You might say, *Well that sounds rather cocky.* I would like to call it confident, not cocky. I don't say this with an attitude of boasting. I want you to know who I am, and why I can speak into your life about marriage. I have been married for a long time to the same amazing man. We have not only succeeded in our marriage, but have raised three children who, although they aren't perfect, all love and serve God.

We have pastored our church for over 30 years, and we are both as strong for Jesus today as the day we married. We are solid and we have the wisdom that comes from living as solid Christians for a very long time.

Who Do You Listen To?

The reason I started off this chapter with my bold statement was to challenge you to seriously think about who you listen to. Be wise, and don't let just anyone speak into your marriage. Many of us have foolishly followed the trends of the popular media; we've bought, read and believed whatever the current guru is saying. I want to shout it from the rooftops: women, quit reading all those books! Don't listen to people who teach about marriage, yet have been married two, three, four, five or ten times or they are just living with somebody. Even worse, we get marriage advice from someone who has never been married.

Don't get me wrong, there are some wonderful books out there on marriage and family, and we should be reading them. However, just because a doctor wrote a book on marriage, does not mean he knows anything. Sometimes, they have been married two or three times themselves; they should be *reading* a book on marriage, not *writing one*. Check your source. Don't listen to a person just because they call themselves an expert. Make an educated decision about who will speak into your marriage.

Let's talk about our *marriage shoes* now. To me these shoes are beautiful, glittery, high heeled, white, pure, and wonderful. Although these are the type of shoe we would wear for our wedding, over the life of our marriage we will need so much more than these amazing shoes. Our *marriage shoes* are really all of the shoes combined. They should be the stomping boots, sneakers, flip flops, high heels, designer shoes, nursing shoes...all wrapped up into one. Our marriage relationship has so many facets to it. I believe marriage is our most significant earthly relationship. It is the one relationship that can strengthen our destiny of walking in God's purpose or it can walk us down a pathway of challenges and problems.

The Real You

In a successful marriage, all the parts of who we are will be engaged. Every shoe is linked to the whole of who we are. An example would be our *slipper shoes:* to me these represent the fact that the man you marry needs to know the real you. Our slippers may be a little worn out, comfortable, not very fancy – but they represent us in our most relaxed moments. They represent our vulnerability...openness...honesty.

We can't wear our slipper shoes all the time. In working towards a great marriage, we don't want to become complacent. Many ladies get the ring on their guy's finger and then let themselves go. They get lazy and forget to keep themselves looking good! So, in addition to our slippers, we've also got to put on our *stiletto shoes.* Remember to put on those shoes that sparkle, glitter and are totally beautiful. Not because it changes whether or not our husband loves us. But, because we value our marriage and we do not take our relationship lightly.

We don't want to become *complacent* in our relationship, so we won't take our husband for granted, or allow him to take us for granted either.

Becoming complacent is the death of many a formerly great marriage. Since we want to give the very best of who we are to our husbands, we need to let them see all the aspects of who we are. We cannot be afraid of letting them see all the shoes in our closet – from the fancy to the plain – they are all valuable.

Slip Into Your Loafers

Let's explore a few more shoes as they relate directly to the marriage relationship. Our *loafers* are the first shoe in our marriage closet. No, loafers are not our lazy boy recliner shoes. To me, our loafers are the everyday pair of shoes we can throw on with our jeans – we slip on this shoe as we just *live our life*. These shoes are so important; they are durable, stable and rather plain. The loafer shoes are not all fancy or glittery – they slip on easily and are our most comfortable shoe. They fit us well, because we spend much of our time in them.

The *loafer shoe* represents our character and is about the fact that we are stable women who love Jesus and love our husbands. We are stable as women of prayer and as wise moms. Stable in that we love our church, love people and love to serve and give. Our loafer shoes reflect the part of us which loves and is kind towards those God has placed in our life.

Some women go into marriage and want to wear their glittery shoes all the time. They crave attention and always require a lot of admiration. There is a sense of selfishness about them; it's all about what they want and need. That kind of selfishness will never produce a great marriage. Great marriages are established on a foundation of give and take; not take, take, and take some more. We have a commitment of respect and caring for one another that goes beyond, *it's all about me.*

One of the most important cornerstones of our marriage is the mission of *living life with purpose*. Casey and I walked into our marriage with a vision to serve God and help people. We were both committed to what we believed God had called us to do. There was no hesitation or discussion about *if* we would serve God; we had made the commitment together to serve God. Our marriage was set on the foundation of God being at the center of our new home. We have kept that commitment all of our married life.

For the Single Girls

Single girls - I want to take a minute to talk just to you. First, make sure you hear from God before you make a commitment to marry that man. Don't date a guy who doesn't have the same commitment to Jesus and the kind of character you have. *Don't settle!* So many girls today allow the guys to treat them like their momma. If a guy doesn't have a job, he's not ready to be in a relationship. If he can't take care of himself, he sure won't be able to take care of you and a family. I've heard girls tell me, *Yeah, he's got 12 kids with 12 different moms, but he's got a really good heart.* Please, value yourself more than to let that kind of guy into your life. You are worth so much more! Before you date a guy, you need to see the abundance of his heart by his actions. Let him show you who he is by what he does. He has to be a doer of the Word in order to be a part of your life. He has to be a church guy; not just a guy who says he goes to church. Ask yourself, *Who will he be long term?*

Next, be the kind of woman that you want your future guy to be. If you want to marry a man with certain qualities and characteristics, make sure you have those same characteristics in your life. Do you want a man of integrity and honesty; do you want him to have a servant's heart, and be truly kind? Do you want him to love Jesus and love the church? You will attract what you are. You will have to be whatever it is you want in your future husband.

Get Out Your Exercise Shoes!

Another key pair of shoes in our marriage relationship is our *exercise shoes*. I know, you think I'm going to talk about physical exercise, but that's not why we put these *exercise shoes* on. I am talking about being a woman who disciplines herself even when she doesn't feel like being disciplined. I am referring to being disciplined enough to only use kind words, when we want to tell them what we really think! I'm talking about having the ability to keep ourselves in check, when instead we want to just let ourselves be totally out of control.

Proverbs teaches us that no husband wants to live with a whiny, complaining wife. *Better to dwell in a corner of a housetop, than in a house shared with a contentious woman,* (Proverbs 21:9); And again the Bible says, *Better to dwell in the wilderness, than with a contentious and angry woman* (Proverbs 21:19).

There is a reason God had to put something like that in the Bible. He knows how we as women can let our emotions rule our mouths! It is because we lack discipline. Many women have a complete lack of control over their mouths. We speak whatever words come into our heads; and we are out of control in the things we say to our husband. If we feel like being mad, we let loose and just say whatever we want to. Once we are married, we think, *I've got my man. I can talk and act however I want!* We use our whiny, complaining, you're-not-good-enough words to the one person we should treat the best. Let's learn to be disciplined in how we speak. Death and life are in the power of your tongue. *Death and life are in the power of the tongue, and those who love it shall eat its fruit* (Proverbs 18:21).

I had to make a serious choice in the area of how I was going to communicate. I was raised in an environment which thrived on a sarcastic type of humor. The words we used had a sarcastic bent to them and for me that was normal. It wasn't a big deal to put someone down or joke in a mean way. Maybe that is true in your home, also.

Learn To Speak Life-Giving Words

It wasn't long after I was saved that I met Casey at Bible school. As we began dating, God opened my eyes to my habit of talking sarcastically. I really saw how talking this way could be very hurtful. I thought, *Is this what I want to be like in 20 years?* I looked at our brand new relationship and thought; *do I want the seeds of all that negativity to grow up in our life?* I could visualize a big orchard filled with dead trees. Those trees were all wilted and ugly, and had no beautiful fruit growing on them. I made a decision that I have never regretted. I learned how to speak life-words. As I began to catch myself saying something sarcastic, I would trade those words for words of life. I want you to hear this loud and clear: LEARN TO SPEAK LIFE-GIVING WORDS! Learn how to speak words of encouragement; learn how to speak kindly. Learn how to build others up with your words. Learn how to give love with your words. *And walk in love, as Christ also has loved us and given Himself for us, an offering and a sacrifice to God for a sweet-smelling aroma* (Ephesians 5:2).

The Bible is full of wisdom about the power of our words. I don't think there is anything more encouraging than someone speaking kind words to us. Throughout Proverbs, we are taught how we should speak. This amazing book of the Bible is full of verses about loving and kindness; it is filled with wisdom about gentleness of the heart and putting other people above ourselves.

When I first saw these scriptures they were so contrary to my way of thinking, and so it is to the way many people think. We often speak in such a negative way towards our husbands. The sarcastic TV shows that many of us watch are teaching us how to communicate in a damaging way to our mates and about our mates. There is so much sarcasm and meanness in the way we talk to one another. We see it everywhere, men talking about their wives, *Oh yeah; I left the old nag at home.* We hear women talking about their husbands, *Oh yeah, my husband, he can't do anything right.* We allow ourselves to keep these negative views about our husbands and we have repeatedly, repeatedly, repeatedly said *relationship killing words* over them.

It's Never Too Late

Since we have planted horrible words into our marriage, through the years we have created something we never wanted or expected to have. The good news is: it is never too late. We can make the decision to be disciplined in how we speak right now. We can put on our *exercise shoes* at any time. The thing about successful exercising is this: we exercise when we don't want to. That's brilliant isn't it? That one concept separates the success of exercise from the failure. Successful people exercise when they don't want to and the failures say, *Oh, it is just too hard.* They simply decide it is too hard and they don't do it. We see the result of that decision in our exercise programs and in our marriages.

If you have been foolish in exalting yourself, or if you have devised evil, put your hand over your mouth (Proverbs 30:32). This verse gives us a practical lesson in how to change the words we speak. Sometimes we just have to physically put our hand over our mouth! We decide what kind of words we will allow to come out of our mouths.

It's not a onetime choice to speak life-giving words. I made the decision years ago when Casey and I started dating; but I still need to keep making that decision every day. There is a temptation to drift into our old ways, especially as we grow older. We must daily practice our decision to speak life over our husband and our marriage. See the positive qualities in your husband and tell him what you see.

Our Beautiful Stiletto Shoes

Let's talk next about our beautiful *stiletto shoes.* These shoes are all sparkly and shiny, and to me, they represent the beauty of really taking care of ourselves. Having pride in who we are as women. We have become relaxed in our culture today. We feel it is okay to just throw on our old gray sweats and our big old T-shirt and head out to the mall...or to the movies...or anywhere. Wearing our hair in a *straight back* pony tail (I mean just slicked back in an old rubber band kind of pony tail) with our T-shirt, which is too big for us and the wrong bra, so our chest hangs down to our knees. It is just not very flattering.

Many of us wear our old tennis shoes with an outfit that is all dirty and wrinkled. Guess what? That is just laziness on our part. You might say, *Yeah, but I don't have enough money.* We can all go to a nice used clothing store and buy better clothes than that. I shopped at a store like that all of my years growing up. Then, I learned how to sew. I used to make all my own clothes, because I could not afford to buy them.

When people say, *I just can't afford it,* I disagree. There are creative ways to get what you need in your life. We can all make sure our clothes smell nice, are clean, and fit us properly. I know there are times we wear those big old sweats because we have been overeating and have gained a bazillion pounds. We need to discipline ourselves and get back into shape so that we can be healthy and attractive to our husband.

What Do You *Really* Weigh?

Many of us were married at our *little girl weight*. By that, I mean we were very young and had the body of a teenager when we were first married. Sadly, we try to get back to that weight all of our adult life. We need to get that number out of our minds; we are never going to weigh that again. That was not our *real* weight. That weight is not the set-point weight that is good for us now. We need to get that number out of our imagination. All of us have a set-point weight that we can be healthy at; one that we can look good at.

On the other hand, some of us have a whole new number in our minds and it is nothing close to our newlywed weight. As we have gotten older, we have let ourselves add on more and more weight. We have bought into the lie that the older we get, the heavier and more out of shape we naturally become. We need to discipline ourselves and get back to a healthy weight and stay there. We need to make sure we aren't so overweight that we can't do anything in life. Some of us need to put on our real *exercise shoes* and shed a few pounds. Start working out a little bit. Eat a little bit less and learn how to eat a little bit healthier.

Every day make sure you look good for your husband. When you are getting ready for your day, make sure your clothes look right on you. On purpose learn what colors look best on you, and then wear those colors. Make sure your clothes are the right size for your body. Don't grow lazy in presenting yourself as a beautiful woman who knows how to take care of herself. Your husband will appreciate the effort, and you will reap the benefits.

It's Not About Money!

Another way we put on our *stiletto shoes* is by learning how to take care of our hair and our make-up. We don't have to always have our hair done fancy, but it should be clean, tidy and look as good as possible on us. Learn how to put on a little bit of makeup. Some of us don't want to wear a lot of makeup and I understand that. We all have different tastes and styles; but the point is, we all have to do *something*. It's not hard to figure out what we like and what to do for ourselves to look the best we can look. There are makeup counters offering free make-overs at every large department store in every mall. Stop and ask some questions. Invest in yourself and be the best *you* can be!

Who can find a virtuous wife? For her worth is far above rubies...She is not afraid of snow for her household, For all her household is clothed with scarlet. She makes tapestry for herself; Her clothing is fine linen and purple. Her husband is known in the gates, When he sits among the elders of the land (Proverbs 31:10 & Proverbs 31:21-23).

Do the best you can for yourself wherever you are at in life. Take a hard look at yourself and do what you can to improve how you look. You are presenting yourself to your husband as his virtuous woman. Do you look like his queen? Do you care for yourself as if you are royalty? The virtuous woman in Proverbs 31 dressed herself in purple and fine linen. These verses communicate the value God places on how we are to take care of ourselves.

Hear this loud! This is not about how much money you can spend on yourself. In taking care of ourselves, some of us are going to love shopping at Target. Some of us are going to love shopping at Neiman Marcus. Where we shop is not what matters. What matters is knowing we are worth the time, the effort and the investment – because we love ourselves and we love our mate. We are sowing into our marriage when we take care of ourselves.

Oh Yeah – Let's Go Shoeless!

Our next shoe is actually...*go shoeless.* Yes, we are going to talk about it – Sex! The intimacy of a sexual relationship in marriage is extremely important. It is not something we can neglect; not if we want to have a long, successful marriage.

It might be time for some of us to go back and read the chapter on getting our *boxing shoes* on. We may need to deal with our past in order to move into our future. I'm completely serious; without dealing with the past and the forgiveness we need, we cannot experience the freedom of sexual intimacy as God intended it. Do what you must to give and receive forgiveness from your past. Only then will you be able to walk into your marriage in an open, vulnerable way.

The basis for all sexual intimacy in marriage is – *naked and not ashamed.* When God created man, He found that Adam was not complete being alone. So, God created Eve, and gave her to Adam as a helpmate; she was to be his partner, his wife. God says they were naked and they were not ashamed. *And they were both naked, the man and his wife, and were not ashamed* (Genesis 2:25).

There are many scriptures about the intimacy of marriage, but I think this verse in Genesis says it the very best. It gives a great understanding of the intimacy of marriage. Nobody else has that place in our life; only with our mate are we to be vulnerable and open on this level. Nobody else should experience the intimacy of that nakedness; the place of vulnerability and innocence that happens in our marriage relationship.

Naked and Not Ashamed

Naked and not ashamed carries such a strong message to us as married couples. If we walk in shame from our past, we must deal with it. We must take accountability for our lives in order to have the openness and freedom we need to give ourselves completely. Some of us come out of tremendous histories; we had sex with everybody you can imagine and now carry the guilt and shame of that.

God wants to heal you right now. He doesn't want you to wait. He wants you to get healed from the mistakes of your past. Yes, you made some bad choices. You have done some stupid things. Jesus was talking to the woman at the well – this woman had been married five times, and the man she was with right then was not her husband. She was living in sin. But, Jesus didn't hold her past against her. He looked at her and said, *Sweetheart, I accept you. I love you and I forgive you.*

> *A woman of Samaria came to draw water. Jesus said to her, 'Give Me a drink.' For His disciples had gone away into the city to buy food. Then the woman of Samaria said to Him, How is it that You, being a Jew, ask a drink from me, a Samaritan woman? For Jews have no dealings with Samaritans. Jesus answered and said to her, If you knew the gift of God, and who it is who says to you, 'Give Me a drink,' you would have asked Him, and He would have given you living water* (John 4:7-10).

That is our God's view of your past. To the woman caught in adultery, He said in John 8:11, *When Jesus had raised Himself up and saw no one but the woman, He said to her, "Woman, where are those accusers of yours? Has no one condemned you?" She said, "No one, Lord." And Jesus said to her, "Neither do I condemn you; go and sin no more."* This woman was caught in adultery. Jesus didn't say, *Well, you've done it now! You have no chance to be forgiven. You are just going to have to live with this; it's too much to forgive!* No! He said, *Go and don't sin anymore.* That's it! Don't sin anymore. Don't do things in your marriage that are dishonorable. Get forgiveness in your marriage and start over with a fresh innocence in your life.

Reaching the Mountain Top

In order to *go shoeless* we have to learn how to have a lot of fun. By that I mean, *regularly* have sex. We have to make time to regularly give ourselves to intimacy in our marriage. When I think of regularly – I'm just going to put it like this – there is breakfast, lunch, dinner, and there are snacks. There are hors d'oeuvres, dessert and then the full-course meals in the intimacy of our sexual relationship.

Sometimes we say to our mate, *Yep, we are just having a little hors d'oeuvre. Come on, baby!* And it is fast and furious. Sometimes we are having a full seven-course meal. We are taking time and it is slow and we are reaching for the mountain top. That is what long-term intimacy in marriage is about - the variety of all the special moments shared together, celebrating our love for each other.

Intimacy should be fun. We need to have some laughter in it; because sometimes we are headed for the full-course meal, but ooops! You just had hors d'oeuvre and are done. And your husband wonders, *What?* Why make it a problem. Sometimes things don't go the way we expected or thought they would – there's always next time. Our most intimate moments should be fun. Let's be joyful as we celebrate our marriage and not always be so serious.

There has to be this sense of joy in life. Since I have been married for over 35 years, I have read many relationship books by various great authors. I appreciated the insight from one particular author who said this: As we get older things change and everything doesn't work quite the same way they have in the past. Hey, things are great when we are younger – at 20 and 30 and 40 – everything kind of works in a certain way. But, then we hit 70 and it is not quite the same. We need to keep our sense of humor. We need to keep working together to have fun in the sweet intimacy of our sexual relationship. This is so very, very important in the long-term of our marriage.

What About This? What About That?

Every time Casey and I teach a marriage seminar we always get the same question: *Is this okay? And is that okay?* We keep it pretty simple. Whatever you agree to on your marriage bed is fine; just don't bring anything onto the bed with you. Some people want to watch videos or have items they want to bring into their sexual relationship. I feel those things don't add anything to the true intimacy of the relationship; in fact, they take away from just focusing on our mate.

The best wisdom I can give you in this area of *going shoeless* is this: Keep sex and the celebration of marriage basic and simple. Learn how to appreciate repetitive satisfaction with your mate. Sex is just what it is. God created it to be exactly what He created it to be. Sex is nothing more and nothing less than the amazing moments of special touches and words of love. How are we going to add something new to that? Some say, *I've never felt like this before.* Really?

How long have you been married? Have you been married just a day? Because climaxes are climaxes; orgasms are orgasms and there are mountain tops, and then another mountain top.

Sex is not going to become something different after 20 years of marriage. It is just as amazing. If you have never had an orgasm, you need to figure out what to do to solve that issue in your marriage. Find a great book; initiate some honest conversations with your husband, and work together to get it right. You and he will enjoy the process, and you will have what God wants you to have in the intimacy of your marriage.

Walk with Me

Our marriage closet has just one more shoe to discuss and I'm going to call it the *slipper shoe*. Our *slipper shoe* is all about living our mission in life with our husband. I am talking about comfortably walking together in unity of purpose. I'm not talking about having to do everything exactly the same in order to feel like we are sharing our goals for the future. He likes certain things more than I do, and the same is true for me. Casey likes to golf and I don't like to golf. I tried. I just didn't like it. I *love* to ride my bike. He *likes* to ride his bike, but I love to ride mine. With our *slipper shoe* I'm talking about something more than shared hobbies, I am talking about being in agreement about our mission of life.

Casey would be considered an introvert. I would be considered more extroverted. Although we are very different in our personalities, we are very much the same in our mission of life: our mission of helping people, our mission of supporting the church, our mission of building friendships, and our mission of raising up our children to love God. We are in agreement about our mission to be good parents to our adult children and grandchildren. That is our mission. We have a unity of purpose and we have the same desires and goals.

Even in the midst of our agreement on the basic beliefs of our life, we are not identical. We have great discussions about the different issues which are a part of our everyday life. We don't always agree on every issue, but we are also not walking down two separate pathways. We do not believe two different philosophies of life. It is very important in a marriage to walk with the same basic mission of life. There is a comfort in that. That is why we put on our *slippers shoes;* there is a comfort in knowing that we walk together in agreement. We both have the same concepts of how to serve, how to give and how to live.

One way Casey and I strongly set the foundation of our marriage was, as we were dating, we had many discussions about our future. We would talk about how much we valued building God's house. We talked about the importance of God's call on our lives and of loving each other. We talked about raising a family. We had a very strong, clear-cut sense of purpose for our lives. And we were in agreement about that purpose.

Stay On Course

Sometimes, in a long-term marriage, one or the other gets a little bit distracted – we can get a little bit off course. We can wander in a new direction that is not true to who we want to be or where we really want to go. That does not mean we cannot get back on course. This is why praying for your husband is so vital. We sow into our mates when we pray for them. We, with the help of the Holy Spirit, get ourselves realigned and back on course. It happens to us all; when we are married for a long time we can get slightly unaligned. We have to work at keeping ourselves in line with the vision we have set before ourselves. That's where having two of us together is so valuable; when one is a little bit out of alignment, the other one is right there praying and believing. We speak words of life and encouragement, and help one another stay on course.

Marriage is about encouraging and building; it is about strengthening each other. Marriage is about fulfilling our mission and it is about laughter. I just want to throw in a pair of *joker shoes* right now. We must have laughter in our lives. Without laughter we will suffocate under the problems and pressures of life. There are too many issues that happen as we walk together in our marriage relationship; we have to laugh and joke about things that come up. As we keep the sweetness and laughter in our marriage, we will have true success!

CHAPTER ELEVEN

Mercy Feet

Mercy Feet

One of the most difficult pair of shoes I have ever had to put on are my *nursing shoes*. Most of our shoes are fun to wear; but nursing shoes are usually worn only when we are in a time of great need. I see our nursing shoes as practical, sturdy and comfortable; but they usually aren't very pretty. And, dealing with sickness is not very pretty either.

I don't know anyone who gets to go through life without having to deal with sickness and disease. Eventually, we all deal with something. Whether the sickness is in us, or our children, our husband, mother, father, or in-law's, we cannot avoid having to deal with it during our lifetime. We live on a cursed earth and sickness just comes with the territory. Each one of us must face sickness at some point; and when that happens we have to figure out how to put on our *nursing shoes*.

None of us really want to have to put on those nursing shoes. I know there are many amazing men and women who serve in the medical field and love what God has called them to do. They love to wear their nursing shoes!

For most of us regular folks, those are the last pair of shoes we want to pull out of the closet and put on.

Most of us grew up with some sort of illnesses that we dealt with as children. Some even planned to be sick to miss certain days at school; or enjoy the special attention that came when we stayed home all day with mom. That never happened at my house. My mom did not cater to sickness. There were no special foods or drinks, no special treatment. My mom did not play around with sickness in that way. And, I feel that has been a huge benefit to me as an adult.

Put on Your Nursing Shoes

I do remember the first time that, as a brand new mom, my little baby was very sick. He was just so tiny. He had gotten a fever and he was so hot – that burning up kind of hot that no mom ever wants to feel. And I just cried. I remember holding him and crying because my little baby was sick and I felt so vulnerable. (It just amazes me that my firstborn, Caleb, is now all grown up with a baby of his own.)

If you are a mom, you have gone through that type of situation with your own children – and you know what I'm talking about. It is such a hard place to be; knowing we need to put on our *nursing shoes,* but wanting to run from the situation as fast as we can. We don't know what to do. We feel so vulnerable; especially when it comes to someone we love and want to protect. It's harder, in a sense, to put on those nursing shoes for someone else, than to be sick ourselves. We feel helpless; and fear dominates our thoughts.

Fear stands at the door and knocks. It just stands at the door and sometimes it has a gentle knock, but sometimes there is a pounding going on inside of us. It is a relentless pounding that tells us; *it's not going to work, you are going to fail; you are going to lose this person.* It's amazing how quickly the devil will come in with his sly thoughts to bring fear. Remember the *spider in the room?* We can become overwhelmed by the emotions that bombard us; all because we allow fear to dominate us.

Get Out Your Arsenal

When Caleb had that fever, it was the first time I ever had to deal with something like that – and it was overwhelming to me. He was so vulnerable and I felt a tremendous need to protect my baby. Not knowing what else to do, I got out my nursing shoes and went to work. Even though I was fearful and feeling overwhelmed, I got the Word of God working in that situation. I prayed and asked God to heal my son. I spoke healing scriptures over his body. I held him and prayed in the Holy Spirit. I did everything I knew to do for him, including using my arsenal of spiritual weapons.

After over twenty-six years and three children, I've had to put on those *nursing shoes* a few times. Not a lot, and the times that I had to put them on were never easy. But, when the situation called for those shoes, I did put them on. We do what we have to as strong, godly women. As we go through each situation and have victory over sickness, it makes us stronger to face the next thing that comes our way. When we fight the smaller battles with faith and prayer, we make ourselves ready when something bigger comes along.

One of those bigger battles for us came when Casey was diagnosed with hepatitis C a few years ago. We had no idea anything was going on in his body. He took a routine physical in order to get an insurance policy for the church. He had to go for that type of testing because we were building our new building and they had to insure Casey during that process. He didn't have any problems physically or any pain in his body, so we were shocked when his blood work came back and they said, *Oh, sorry, we can't insure you. You didn't pass the physical.*

We were completely stunned by that negative medical report. It was the last thing we were expecting to hear. As we started the process of finding out what was wrong with Casey, I had to put on my *nursing shoes* big time. And so have many of you had to put on your nursing shoes. We all need to ask ourselves, *How will I deal with it when I get a negative medical report?* Either for ourselves or for someone we love. What do we do when someone we love is going through a situation that is heart wrenching and sad.

Fear Will Try to Bowl You Over

When we received the report about Casey, I instantly had an overwhelming sense of fear. I thought, *Oh my goodness – no way – this is my man, this is my one and only.* Fear literally just bowled me over. Never think you will not have a human reaction to that level of shocking news. We are all humans and sometimes our emotions will try to take control of us. The fear will try to control our response to the situation. That is the time we need to be ready with the weapons of our warfare – The Word of God.

After my initial thoughts of shock; I immediately got out my nursing shoes as I decided what kind of woman I was going to be. I knew we would walk through this situation together, and I knew that we would win. We don't get to make a one-time decision of success when it comes to wearing our nursing shoes. Things happen all the time; and we have to get our shoes on and fight every single time. We have to decide – is what God's Word says in I Peter 2:24 true in our life, in every situation? *...who Himself bore our sins in His own body on the tree, that we, having died to sins, might live for righteousness— by whose stripes you were healed* (1 Peter 2:24).

We Fight to Win

Do we really believe by His stripes we were healed? Acts 10:38 says, *...how God anointed Jesus of Nazareth with the Holy Spirit and with power, who went about doing good and healing all who were oppressed by the devil, for God was with Him.* We see the pattern of God's Word from Genesis to Revelation – God loves us and He is our healer. God designed for us to be healthy physically while we live on earth. God's design is that no sickness or disease takes us out before our time. We are all going to leave this earth some time, but we want to make sure it is at the appropriate time; so we have to be ready to fight and win.

Some of us have tragically lost loved ones before their time. I am so sorry. There is nothing worse on earth than losing a loved one; especially at a young age. It is very difficult to get back in the *saddle of faith* and begin believing God again when we have experienced such a painful loss. We must understand that earth-life is full of trials and challenges; and the devil comes to kill, steal and destroy. Always remember, as long as we are on earth, the devil comes daily, moment-by-moment with that one goal in mind. *The thief does not come except to steal, and to kill, and to destroy. I have come that they may have life, and that they may have it more abundantly* (John 10:10). That is his whole agenda – to kill, to steal, and to destroy from every human being on earth.

That means we are in a relentless fight. It's not like he is going to just give up. It would be great if only the evil people got some kind of sickness or disease as pay-back, but that's not how it works. Every one of us is going to have something happen. Let me just say this; *you* are not evil if something bad has happened to you or a loved one. You may have even fought the good fight of faith, but did not get the kind of result you wanted. That does not make you bad; that means the devil is wicked and he is bad.

Set Your Heart at Peace

Yes, we have lost at times. We've had challenges at times. Sometimes a person will go into the hospital with great odds in their favor, and they don't come out. Other times people are hospitalized with unbelievable odds against them, and they come out whole. Why? There are things on earth we will never ever have an answer for. Even though we don't have an answer; we can set our hearts at peace, knowing that God is love and the devil is evil. That is the only answer we have while here on earth. Deuteronomy 29:29 teaches us, *The secret things belong to the Lord our God, but those things which are revealed belong to us and to our children forever, that we may do all the words of this law.*

Although we will never understand everything that happens on earth, our job right now is to put on our *nursing shoes* of faith and say, *I'm going to fight the fight of faith. I'm going to fight for healing. I'm going to believe that the Word of God says, by His stripes I am healed.* Even those who die before their time, ultimately win. As Christians, our loved ones get their healing when they enter Heaven. Even though we miss them terribly here on earth, they are in Heaven with Father God.

Battle Plan

When Casey and I began the battle with hepatitis C, they gave him a 5% chance of beating the disease. The doctors all said only 5% of the people who have fought against this virus were ever able to get rid of it completely. Basically, that meant if he did not get healed, although he would not die suddenly, his life would be shortened. Shortened by how much? Well, we don't know.

He had already had pneumonia several times in his life. He had battled pneumonia four times – with a couple of the times being very serious. Although we did not know it at the time, part of that was due to the sickness in his body. Once we figured out he had hepatitis C, we realized where certain problems had come from. We recognized that he already had reoccurring sickness in his body, which was shortening his life.

As I mentioned, immediately we knew we had to fight and do everything we could to get his body healthy again. We had a very wise friend who was in the medical profession give us a scripture during this time. This scripture became the basis for our fight against this disease. *He who is loose and slack in his work is brother to him who is a destroyer and he who does not use his endeavors to heal himself is brother to him who commits suicide* (Proverbs 18:9 AMP).

That Word resonated within our spirits and we knew that we would go into this fight armed with every means available to us. We were going to use every endeavor to heal Casey as the scripture teaches us. As we researched our options, we found an experimental program for him here in our state. It was through our local university and was pretty tough to get into. Less than 50% of those who entered completed the program because it was very difficult emotionally and physically. Casey and I determined that this was the God-direction for us and we determined to put on our nursing shoes of faith to walk through this together.

As Casey began taking all the drugs and having regular chemotherapy many things began to happen – emotionally and physically. I have to say, this was one of the most challenging periods of my life. I talked earlier about walking in the joy of the Lord and putting on your dancing shoes. I really learned what that meant during this time. Please understand, I would not have been able to succeed at this level of faith if I had not started putting on my nursing shoes when Caleb had a fever as a baby.

Live a Life of Faith

We lived a life of speaking God's Word over ourselves and our family. We were young Christians when we decided to walk by faith daily, so we had been speaking the Word of God for many, many years at this time. When this huge battle came up, we were ready to fight. We spoke the Word of faith daily. Every day we got out the scriptures. We took God's Word and together we developed a confession of healing. We confessed the Word of God every day. Why? There is life in God's Word and in the power of our tongue as we confess it. (You will find a copy of Casey's confession at the end of this chapter).

God's Word will defeat the fear which wants to come against us. Hearing ourselves say those words over and over again helped us to not only keep our faith, but actually built our faith. Fear will want to dominate us and our situation. If those feelings of fear get the best of us, we will be defeated. We have to decide if we will allow our own thoughts to control our world. If we do, fear will overcome us and we will begin to speak, *It's impossible; this sickness is just too big; I will never win!* We will begin to walk in a downward spiral of disaster, instead of faith.

As we began to fight the fight of faith, we got other people in agreement around us. We got our elders and our pastors to pray for us. We got our friends in agreement. We eventually stood up in front of our congregation and asked the church family, *Will you agree with us in faith?* People would stretch their hands out towards us and pray for Casey in accordance with the Bible. Again, this is why being a part of the church family is so important; there is strength as we walk together in agreement. *Again I say to you that if two of you agree on earth concerning anything that they ask, it will be done for them by My Father in heaven* (Matthew 18:19).

We won the battle for Casey's healing eleven months later, as we received a letter from his doctors documenting his total healing from hepatitis C. It was not an easy win, but we made it by proclaiming our faith and walking according to all we knew to do.

Not Every Victory Happens on Earth

Sadly, not every person will experience victory over sickness and disease while living on the earth. My mom was diagnosed with cancer when she was 68 years old. My mom also went through chemotherapy and did all she could; including fighting spiritually. We did everything we knew to do, yet she only lived two more years on earth. She received long-term victory by walking into heaven, but she was only 70 years old.

One thing I really regret is this: my mom knew something was wrong with her, but instead of facing and dealing with the pain in her body, she ignored it. She ignored the pain for so long that by the time we began the fight, the disease already dominated her body. I wish she had sought help sooner.

I was honestly shocked when my mom died. I wasn't prepared for it to end that way. She was too young to leave earth. My grandparents had both lived very long lives on earth. They were both almost one hundred years old when they went to be with the Lord. Based on that, I expected my mom to live longer.

I have experienced both sides of fighting the fight of faith; one of earth victory and one of heaven victory. I want you to understand, although we fight, we don't always know what is on other side of our situation. We don't always get the results we think we should, and so we can become disheartened.

Some of you are dealing with this kind of issue in your life right now. Just as I had to deal with the questions of what happened, so are you. I thought I had my nursing shoes on. Even though we did not win earth victory for my mom; and you may have not won in your situation, I can only say, we have to fight the fight of faith. We will not see every situation clearly from our position here on earth.

We Know in Part

The Bible teaches us that we only know part of the story here on earth. *For now we see in a mirror, dimly, but then face to face. Now I know in part, but then I shall know just as I also am known* (1 Corinthians 13:12). We won't always understand everything. Deuteronomy also says the secret things belong to God. *The secret things belong to the Lord our God, but those things which are revealed belong to us and to our children forever, that we may do all the words of this law* (Deuteronomy 29:29).

I don't understand everything and I'm not going to pretend that I do.

What I do know is this; God says that by His stripes I am healed. *...who Himself bore our sins in His own body on the tree, that we, having died to sins, might live for righteousness—by whose stripes you were healed* (1 Peter 2:24).

I do know that the Bible says that the devil comes to steal, kill and destroy. *The thief does not come except to steal, and to kill, and to*

destroy. I have come that they may have life, and that they
may have it more abundantly (John 10:10).

I do know that we are in a fight of faith.

Fight the good fight of faith, lay hold on eternal life, to which
you were also called and have confessed the good confession
in the presence of many witnesses (1 Timothy 6:12).

Lose a Battle, Win the War!

Yes, we are in a fight. Does everybody always win? No. We may not win every battle – but we do win the war. If we lose this battle on earth at a young age and we know Jesus – we still win because we are in Heaven. That is definitely a win/win situation! We just have to look at it from that perspective. Going to Heaven to be with Jesus is a win/win. We cannot go into the depths of despair when we don't get the answer we would like. It was still a win/win when my mom left earth life at a young age. I wish she would have lived longer, but she ultimately won because she is in Heaven. Now she is living totally pain-free.

Would I have liked my mom to be with us longer on earth? Of course I would, but that is not what happened. Therefore, I choose to rejoice in the fact that she is in Heaven. We each have the choice to decide how we are going to respond to the problems we face.

Daily Speak God's Word

Healing isn't only about the extreme cases of sickness. Healing is for the time my Caleb had that fever as a baby. Healing is for when our child falls down and skins his knee. Healing is for when we wake up sneezing or have an allergy attack or we just plain have a headache. How do we deal with the day-to-day sickness that tries to come against us? We daily speak God's Word. I can't say enough about how significant and important this is. Unfortunately, some of us get hit with something serious in our life, but we have no strength built up to believe for healing because we have not sown God's healing Word into our hearts.

I remember way back in the beginning of my Christian walk when I first heard the scripture, *by His stripes we are healed.* I meditated on that verse and eventually I realized, wait a minute, He is talking about me. At that time, I was having headaches all the time, and I thought, *I'll just take an aspirin.* But, as I meditated on God's Word, it came to me, *I'm not going to die if I don't take an aspirin.* Rather than running to the aspirin bottle, I decided to take God's Word instead.

I decided to exercise my faith in that particular area. I realized I could build up my faith in God's healing power by pressing myself to believe His Word. By pushing myself and believing in this particular area, I began putting on my *nursing shoes* of healing. I began to fight back when sickness and pain tried to get on my body, by attacking it with the prayer of faith. I fought by confessing God's Word over myself. I decided the next time I had a headache to do it all again. Every time that pain tried to come on my body I began to say, *By His stripes I'm healed.*

I began to speak God's promises. *He sent His word and healed them, And delivered them from their destructions* (Psalm 107:20). We need to know God's promises. We need to find scriptures on healing and begin to speak the Word over ourselves. We also need to teach our children the value of praying God's Word over themselves. We all need to learn how to speak healing over our bodies; that is how we will stay healthy and whole.

Start with the Small Things

As I began experimenting with my new found knowledge of God's Word, I chose something that wasn't life threatening. If I didn't get healed of my headache – what did it matter? I wasn't going to keel over and die. So, instead of running to the easy fix of the medicine bottle, when pain came on my body, I began to declare God's promises for healing. Each time I did this, I became stronger and stronger, until I no longer had headaches

Let me say this about healing and our children – children have little *ouchies* from the earliest of age. We can make them a big deal, which makes sickness a time of great attention and affection, or we can treat those times of *little hurts* as no big deal. We are training our children by how we deal with the little hurts of life. Most mamas get all emotional and worried when their child gets hurt; which makes the child cry more. The child cries more, and we get more worried about whatever is going on. Instead, stay calm; make it no big deal. If one of mine was playing and fell down, I always told them, *You're fine, go ahead and keep playing with your friends.* If it was a little more serious, I would very simply pray for them and then send them on their way. The Bible says believers lay hands on the sick and they shall recover.

> *...And these signs will follow those who believe: In My name they will cast out demons; they will speak with new tongues; they will take up serpents; and if they drink anything deadly, it will by no means hurt them; they will lay hands on the sick, and they will recover* (Mark 16:17-18).

Are we doing that? When our friend says, *I'm feeling really bad.* Are we saying, *You know what? Let me just say a quick little prayer for you.* We don't have to yell, *Hey, God!* Just put your hand on their shoulder and say, *I speak healing in Jesus' Name.* It releases the power of God within them to bring healing into their life.

Don't Get Stuck on Why

Now the devil is always going to try to come to steal and kill and destroy from us. He is always going to try to make us afraid to pray for our friends, or to pray for ourselves. He will try to make us remember every little incident that didn't work the way we thought it should. When we don't fully understand something just say, *You know what? I don't understand everything and that's okay.* We don't understand why one gets sick and another doesn't. We don't know why one is healed and one is not. That is earth-life and that is the devil's work of coming to kill, steal and destroy.

Many Christians ask the question, *Yeah, but why didn't God...?* I don't know. Do you know? I'm not going to try to answer all those questions because, I'm not God. You can't answer those questions; you're not God either. That is like a kindergartner asking a brilliant mathematician, *Why don't I understand everything that you understand?* And that brilliant mathematician saying, *It's just not possible, sweetheart.* We would all want to say to that little kindergartner, *You will eventually understand a lot more, but right now you have the understanding of a kindergartner.* So, as we grow in knowledge of God's Word, we will grow to understand His ways and live in the healing He has provided for us.

Personally, that gives me peace. I feel comforted that our God, The One who created the heavens and the earth; Who created the stars in the sky, and all the beautiful mountains; Who made the depths of the ocean and the colors of the fields of flowers; that Creator, who shows His love by the beauty of His creation, is our God.

We can choose what we are going to believe for. We can choose what kind of shoes that we are going to wear. We choose to wear all shoes He has given us – the nursing shoes – the dancing shoes – our stomping boots – our marriage shoes – our boxing shoes – and even our barefoot prayer non-shoes! We have been given so much by our Father God; how can we not just love Him more and more as we continue to *Shoes Wisely* to follow Him!

Casey's Healing Confession

I am healed and whole in the name of Jesus, from the top of my head to the souls of my feet. Every bone, organ, muscle, nerve and cell of my body functions perfectly.

Jesus bore my sickness and carried my disease when He died on the Cross and made the way for me to be saved, healed and blessed of God. He has taken sickness away from me. Through His stripes I was healed.

Pain or sickness have no place in me. I refuse to allow pain or sickness in my life. I am born of God and filled with the Spirit of God. The same Spirit that raised Jesus from the dead quickens (makes whole) my mortal body.

In Jesus' name I walk in health, wholeness and divine life.

How to Be Born Again

Every person on earth has sinned and is in need of a personal relationship with God. Romans 3:23 says that *all have sinned and fall short of the glory of God.*

To have a personal relationship, you must believe in the Lord Jesus Christ as your Lord and Savior. According to John 3:16, it is through believing in Jesus that we receive eternal life: *For God so loved the world that He gave His only begotten Son, that whoever believes in Him should not perish but have everlasting life.*

When you are born again, you can know God and have everlasting life. John 3:3 says, *Jesus answered and said to him, 'Most assuredly, I say to you, unless one is born again, he cannot see the kingdom of God.'*

Being born again is the gift of God. It cannot be earned, and you cannot achieve it on your own. Romans 6:23 says, *For the wages of sin is death, but the gift of God is eternal life in Christ Jesus our Lord.*

Ephesians 2:8-9 makes it clear: *For it is by grace you have been saved, through faith—and this not from yourselves, it is the gift of God—not by works, so that no one can boast.*

When you are born again, you receive Jesus as your Lord and Master, and you commit yourself to follow His Word (the Bible). Romans 10:9-10 says, *That if you confess with your mouth the Lord Jesus and believe in your heart that God has raised Him from the dead, you will be saved. For with the heart one believes unto righteousness, and with the mouth confession is made unto salvation.*

I John 2:3 tells us it is a commitment: *Now by this we know that we know Him, if we keep His commandments.*

If you are ready to make this life-changing commitment, then pray according to Romans 10:9-10:

> *God, I come to You in the Name of Jesus. I ask You to come into my life. I confess with my mouth that Jesus is my Lord and I believe in my heart that You have raised Him from the dead. I turn my back on sin and I commit to follow You for the rest of my life. I thank You, Father, for saving me!*

Welcome to the family of Christ! You are now born again, forgiven and on your way to heaven. You are a new creation in Christ Jesus. II Corinthians 5:17 says, *Therefore, if anyone is in Christ, he is a new creation; old things have passed away; behold, all things have become new.*

Yet this is only the beginning of your new life as a Christian. As you study God's Word and apply its truths to your life, you will renew your mind and grow as a Christian.

Romans 12:1-2 says, *I beseech you therefore, brethren, by the mercies of God, that you present your bodies a living sacrifice, holy, acceptable to God, which is your reasonable service. And do not be conformed to this world, but be transformed by the renewing of your mind, that you may prove what is that good and acceptable and perfect will of God.*

Become a part of a church where the Word of God is preached in truth, and you can be encouraged by other believers. Hebrews 10:25 says, *Not forsaking the assembling of ourselves together, as is the manner of some, but exhorting one another, and so much the more as you see the Day approaching.*

If doubts or fears come to your mind that you are not truly born again, reject them and realize that God's Word is what your salvation is based on, not what you think or feel.

Romans 10:9-10, the verses you based your prayer on, say, *That if you confess with your mouth the Lord Jesus and believe in your heart that God has raised Him from the dead, you will be saved. For with the heart one believes unto righteousness, and with the mouth confession is made unto salvation.*

Part of the Christian walk is to publicly acknowledge your decision through being baptized in water. John the Baptist, baptized Jesus in the Jordan River. Jesus desires that those who accept Him be baptized. Acts 10:48 says, *And he commanded them to be baptized in the name of the Lord.*

To help you succeed on this earth as a Christian, God has also given you the gift of the Holy Spirit. He is your helper.

Being Filled With the Holy Spirit

The Holy Spirit is your comforter and teacher. He has been given to you to help you in your everyday life. John 14:26 says, *But the Helper, the Holy Spirit, whom the Father will send in My name, He will teach you all things, and bring to your remembrance all things that I said to you.*

The Holy Spirit will give you the power to be a strong witness for Jesus. Acts 1:8 says, *But you shall receive power when the Holy Spirit has come upon you; and you shall be witnesses to Me in Jerusalem, and in all Judea and Samaria, and to the end of the earth.*

When you are filled with the Holy Spirit, you can speak in other tongues for the purpose of prayer, prophesying, worship and personal edification. Acts

2:4 says, *And they were all filled with the Holy Spirit and began to speak with other tongues, as the Spirit gave them utterance.*

The Holy Spirit is for every born again person. You don't have to wait or work to receive Him. Acts 2:38-39 tells us, *Then Peter said to them, 'Repent, and let every one of you be baptized in the name of Jesus Christ for the remission of sins; and you shall receive the gift of the Holy Spirit. For the promise is to you and to your children, and to all who are afar off, as many as the Lord our God will call.'*

When you receive the Holy Spirit and speak in other tongues, your mind will not understand anything you are saying. It will sound useless and foolish to you, but you are speaking mysteries to God, not to yourself or to other people.

I Corinthians 14:2 says, *For he who speaks in a tongue does not speak to men but to God, for no one understands him; however, in the spirit he speaks mysteries.*

Speaking in tongues is an act of your will. God gives you the ability to do it, but He will not force you or do it for you. I Corinthians 14:14-15 says, *For if I pray in a tongue, my spirit prays, but my understanding is unfruitful. What is the conclusion then? I will pray with the spirit, and I will also pray with the understanding. I will sing with the spirit, and I will also sing with the understanding.*

If you ask for the Holy Spirit in faith, God the Father will give Him to you: *If you then, being evil, know how to give good gifts to your children, how much more will your heavenly Father give the Holy Spirit to those who ask Him!* (Luke 11:13).

Would you like to receive the Holy Spirit today?

If so, pray according to Luke 11:13, asking God to fill you with the Holy Spirit:

Father, I come to You in the Name of Jesus. I ask You to fill me with Your Holy Spirit. I receive Him from You and according to the Bible I will now pray in other tongues as the Spirit gives me the utterance. Thank You, Father!

After praying this prayer asking God to fill you, pray confidently in other tongues. As you pray regularly in other tongues, it will build you up and charge up your spirit man. Jude 1:20 says, ***But you, beloved, building yourselves up on your most holy faith, praying in the Holy Spirit.***

How to Recommit Your Life to Christ

If you have made Jesus the Lord of your life, but have fallen away from living a Christian life, you can recommit your life to God. Simply confess and admit your sin to Him. He is faithful to forgive.

I John 1:9 says, ***If we confess our sins, He is faithful and just to forgive us our sins and to cleanse us from all unrighteousness.***

Once you confess your sins and receive God's forgiveness, thank Him for forgiving you. He is a just and loving God.

Next, seek out a Bible-believing and Bible-teaching church. You need to be trained in the Word of God so you can grow in your Christian walk.

—Casey and Wendy Treat

For information on teaching materials by

Casey and Wendy Treat contact us at:

P.O. Box 98800 Seattle, WA 98198 or call 1-800-644-4446

order online at: www.caseytreat.com and www.wendytreat.com

Wendy invites you to follow her on Twitter @wendytreat

or become a Fan of Wendy Treat on Facebook

For additional tools, tips, and training, go to shoeswisely.org